Masterpiece
SHOWCASE™

Editorial Director: DONNA ROBERTSON
Design Director: FRAN ROHUS
Production/Photography Director: ANGE VAN ARMAN

EDITORIAL
Senior Editor: JANET TIPTON
Editor: KRIS KIRST
Composing Editors: JEANNE AUSTIN, JUDY CROW,
JAIMIE DAVENPORT, KAREN WANN
Assistant Graphics Editor: REBECCA MOEHNKE
Copy Editor: SALWAY SABRI

PRODUCTION
Production Manager/Book Design: DEBBY KEEL
Special Graphics/Cover Design: COY LOTHROP
Color Specialist: BETTY RADLA
Production Coordinator: GLENDA CHAMBERLAIN

PHOTOGRAPHY
Photography Manager: SCOTT CAMPBELL
Photographers: RUSSELL CHAFFIN, KEITH GODFREY
Photography Coordinator/Stylist: RUTH WHITAKER
Assistant Photo Stylist: BETH AUGUSTINE

PRODUCT DESIGN
Design Coordinator: TONYA FLYNN

BUSINESS
C.E.O: JOHN ROBINSON
Vice President/Marketing: GREG DEILY

CREDITS
Sincerest thanks to all the designers, manufacturers and other professionals whose dedication
has made this book possible. Special thanks to Quebecor Printing Book Group, Kingsport, TN.

Library of Congress Cataloging-in-Publication Data
ISBN: 1-57367-104-5
First Printing: 1998
Library of Congress Catalog Card Number: 98-66978

Published and Distributed by
The Needlecraft Shop, LLC, Big Sandy, Texas 75755
Printed in the United States of America.

Dear Friends,

Masterpiece Showcase *brings together some of the best plastic canvas designers in the United States. Showcasing the works of each individual artist, this book puts the spotlight on several of the multi-talented people responsible for the rise in popularity and new expression of the age-old craft of needlepoint.*

Prompted by Design Director for The Needlecraft Shop, *Fran Rohus, each designer contributed a fresh sampling of new ideas, all of which are sure to become the collectible handwork keepsakes of tomorrow. The finished projects arrived in our design studio from all over the country and were set out for inspection with each artist's work grouped together on long tables. What fun we had browsing admiringly through each special collection!*

Why don't you join us? Tour the pages of Masterpiece Showcase *as you would an art gallery – pause to notice the specific strokes and touches that make each designer's work a reflection of his or her unique and ever-so-personal style. Our fun doesn't have to stop at the last page. Are you ready to gather your materials? The creativity of our designers is catching. Let's begin stitching our most-favorite design tonight!*

Janet

Table of Contents

Debbie Tabor

Janelle Giese

Robin Petrina

Mike Vickery

CHAPTER 1

Sandra Miller Maxfield

To plastic canvas enthusiasts, designer Sandra Miller Maxfield is a familiar friend. A professional designer in both plastic canvas and crochet since the late 1980s and full-time designer for *The Needlecraft Shop* since 1993, Sandra continues to delight stitchers with her innovative projects.

Many of Sandra's designs are of a religious nature and express her deep and abiding faith. Many more show her fun-loving side, as her magic needle creates whimsical characters and holiday decorating projects that brighten family homes at traditional gathering times throughout the year. Sandra loves experimenting with new yarns and craft materials, and she really has fun playing with a new computer design program. Her playful imagination and bold use of color make her designs some of the most-stitched projects in the world of plastic canvas.

Her family really gets involved when she designs at home. Sandra's husband, Marvin, has spent countless hours with yarn and needle, bringing many of her ideas to life. When not occupied with a new project, Sandra and Marvin hang up the Gone Fishin' sign and spend time with their grandchildren.

Halloween Friends

SIZE & MATERIALS

Size: 12" x 15⅝".

Materials: 1¼ sheets of 7-count plastic canvas; Two yellow 18mm starflake beads; Two black 4mm round faceted beads; Craft glue or glue gun; Worsted-weight or plastic canvas yarn (for amounts see Color Key).

INSTRUCTIONS

Cutting Instructions:

(Note: Graphs continued on page 10.)
A: For cat body, cut one according to graph.
B: For cat head, cut one according to graph.
C: For bow tie, cut one according to graph.
D: For large pumpkin, cut one according to graph.
E: For small pumpkin, cut one according to graph.
F: For ghost, cut one according to graph.
G: For long leaf, cut one according to graph.
H: For short leaf, cut one according to graph.

Stitching Instructions:

1: Using colors and stitches indicated, work pieces according to graphs; fill in uncoded areas of A and B pieces using black and Continental Stitch. With black for cat body and head, fern for small pumpkin stem, moss for bow tie and with matching colors, Overcast edges of A-H pieces.
2: Using black (Separate into individual plies, if desired.) and Backstitch, embroider mouth on F piece as indicated on graph.
3: Glue one black bead to center of each starflake bead; glue one starflake bead inside each cutout on B.
4: Glue pieces together according to Halloween Friends Assembly Illustration. Hang or display as desired.◙

Halloween Friends Assembly Illustration
(Beads not shown.)

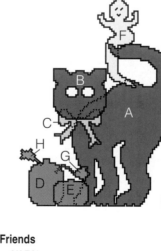

G – Long Leaf
(cut 1)
8 x 17 holes

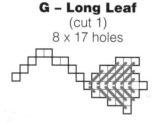

H – Short Leaf
(cut 1)
7 x 12 holes

D – Large Pumpkin
(cut 1) 17 x 23 holes

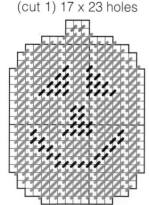

COLOR KEY: Halloween Friends

	Worsted-weight	Nylon Plus™	Need-loft®	YARN AMOUNT
■	Black	#02	#00	42 yds.
	Bt. Orange	#17	#58	8 yds.
	White	#01	#41	7 yds.
	Fern	#57	#23	4 yds.
	Moss	#48	#25	4 yds.
	Pewter	#40	#65	4 yds.
	Bt. Purple	–	#64	3 yds.

STITCH KEY:
— Backstitch/Straight Stitch

Let Halloween guests be welcomed by these frightful four.

Halloween Friends

Instructions & photo on pages 8 & 9.

COLOR KEY: Halloween Friends

	Worsted-weight	Nylon Plus™	Need-loft®	YARN AMOUNT
■	Black	#02	#00	42 yds.
▨	Bt. Orange	#17	#58	8 yds.
▨	White	#01	#41	7 yds.
▨	Fern	#57	#23	4 yds.
▨	Moss	#48	#25	4 yds.
▨	Pewter	#40	#65	4 yds.
■	Bt. Purple	–	#64	3 yds.

STITCH KEY:

— Backstitch/Straight Stitch

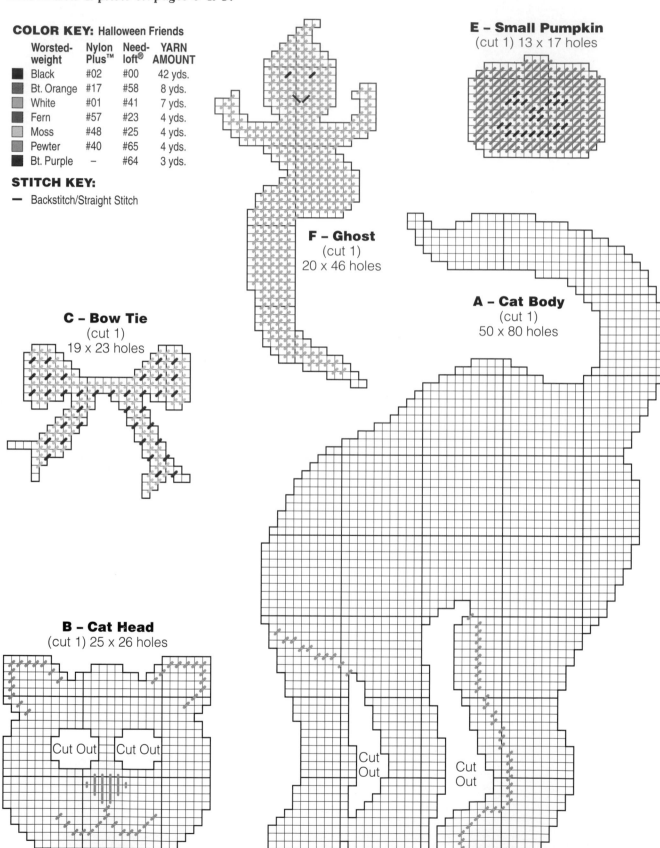

E – Small Pumpkin
(cut 1) 13 x 17 holes

F – Ghost
(cut 1)
20 x 46 holes

A – Cat Body
(cut 1)
50 x 80 holes

C – Bow Tie
(cut 1)
19 x 23 holes

B – Cat Head
(cut 1) 25 x 26 holes

Cut Out   Cut Out

Cut Out

Cut Out

Holiday Glimmer Pals

Instructions on next page

■ Holiday Glimmer Pals

Photo on page 11.

SIZE & MATERIALS

Sizes: Santa is 3⅝" x about 15"; Uncle Sam is 3¾" x about 8½"; Witch is 4½" x about 8½".

Materials: One sheet of 7-count plastic canvas; Scrap of red 7-count plastic canvas; Six 20mm reflective craft disks; Three gold ¾" jingle bells; Two blue stars, two red navette, two blue heart, and two red heart foil-backed acrylic stones (about 10mm size); Quilting thread or monofilament fishing line; Craft glue or glue gun; Worsted-weight or plastic canvas yarn (for amounts see Color Key).

INSTRUCTIONS

Cutting Instructions:

A: For Santa, cut one from clear according to graph.
B: For Uncle Sam, cut one from clear according to graph.
C: For Witch, cut one from clear according to graph.

D: For Witch mouth, cut one from red according to graph.

Stitching Instructions:

1: Using colors and stitches indicated, work A-C pieces according to graphs; with matching colors, Overcast edges.
2: Using white and French Knot, embroider stars on B as indicated on graph.
(Note: Cut sixty-two 15" lengths of white.)
3: For each strand of Santa's beard, thread one 15" strand of white on needle. Run needle from front to back, then from back to front through holes on each side of ◆ bar as indicated; pull ends to even.
(Note: Cut twelve 3" lengths of white.)
4: For each strand of Uncle Sam's beard, repeat Step 3 with 3" strands.
(Note: Cut twelve 4" lengths of black.)
5: For each strand of Witch's hair, repeat Step 3 with 4" strands.
6: For Santa, Uncle Sam and Witch, assemble pieces according to Pals Assembly Diagram. Hang as desired.◉

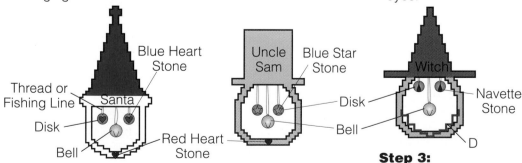

Pals Assembly Diagram
(Beards and hair not shown for clarity.)

Step 1:
Secure bells to thread or fishing line; glue end of lines to center back of hats with bells hanging in center of cutout for noses.

Step 2:
Secure disks to thread or fishing line; glue end of lines to each side of nose string for eyes.

Blue Heart Stone

Uncle Sam

Blue Star Stone

Witch

Thread or Fishing Line

Santa

Disk

Navette Stone

Disk

Bell

D

Bell

Red Heart Stone

Step 4:
Glue one blue heart stone to each Santa disk, one star stone to each Uncle Sam disk and one navette stone to each Witch disk.

Step 3:
Glue one red heart stone to Santa and one to Uncle Sam over beard strands for mouths; glue D to Witch.

A – Santa
(cut 1 from clear)
24 x 50 holes

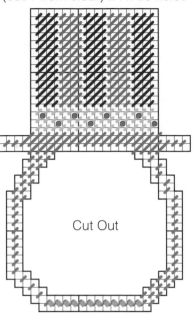

Cut Out

Cut Out

B – Uncle Sam
(cut 1 from clear) 24 x 38 holes

Cut Out

C – Witch
(cut 1 from clear)
30 x 43 holes

Cut Out

COLOR KEY: Holiday Glimmer Pals

Worsted-weight	Nylon Plus™	Need-loft®	YARN AMOUNT
White	#01	#41	34 yds.
Xmas Red	#19	#02	11 yds.
Purple	#21	#46	6 yds.
Bt. Green	–	#61	4 yds.
Flesh Tone	–	#56	4 yds.
Royal	#09	#32	2 yds.
Bt. Orange	#17	#58	1½ yds.
Yellow	#26	#57	1 yd.

STITCH KEY:
- ● French Knot
- ◆ Hair Attachment

D – Witch's Mouth
(cut 1 from red)
9 x 18 holes

Cut around bars carefully.

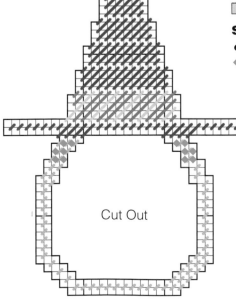
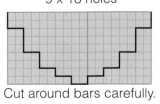

Royal Flush Frames

SIZE & MATERIALS

Size: Each is 8¾" x 10½" with a 2¼" x 2⅞" photo window.

Materials: Three sheets of 7-count plastic canvas; Worsted-weight or plastic canvas yarn (for amounts see Color Key).

INSTRUCTIONS

Cutting Instructions:
For Queen, King and Joker Frames, cut one each according to graphs. (King and Joker graphs on pages 16 & 17.)

according to graphs. (King and Joker graphs on pages 16 & 17.)

COLOR KEY: Royal Flush Frames

	Worsted-weight	Nylon Plus™	Need-loft®	YARN AMOUNT
	White	#01	#41	4 oz.
	Xmas Red	#19	#02	40 yds.
	Black	#02	#00	38 yds.
	Yellow	#26	#57	10 yds.
	Silver	–	#37	6 yds.

STITCH KEY:
— Backstitch/Straight Stitch

Queen
(cut 1) 58 x 70 holes

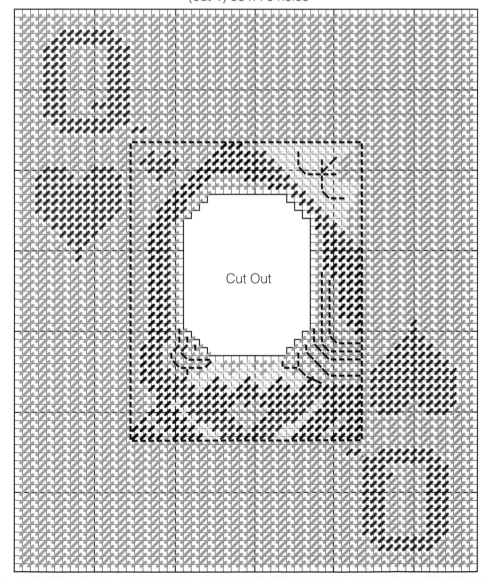

Cut Out

◼ Royal Flush Frames

Continued from page 15.

Stitching Instructions:

1: Using colors and stitches indicated, work pieces according to graphs; with silver for cutout edges of King and with black, Overcast edges of Frames.

2: Using black (Separate into individual plies, if desired.) and Backstitch, embroider detail as indicated on graphs.

3: Secure picture behind cutout, and hang as desired.◉

COLOR KEY: Royal Flush Frames

	Worsted-weight	Nylon Plus™	Need-loft®	YARN AMOUNT
	White	#01	#41	4 oz.
	Xmas Red	#19	#02	40 yds.
	Black	#02	#00	38 yds.
	Yellow	#26	#57	10 yds.
	Silver	–	#37	6 yds.

STITCH KEY:
— Backstitch/Straight Stitch

Joker
(cut 1) 58 x 70 holes

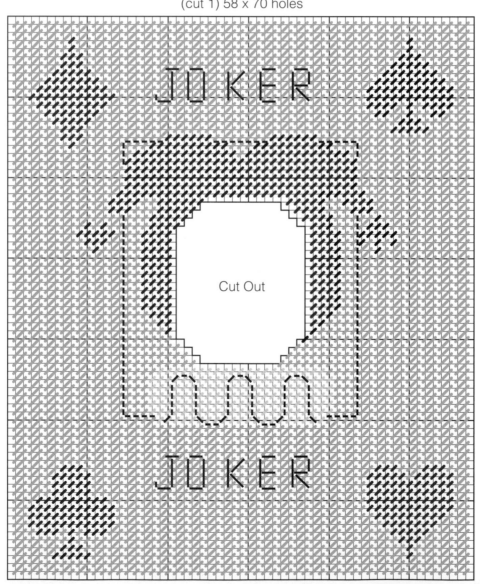

King
(cut 1) 58 x 70 holes

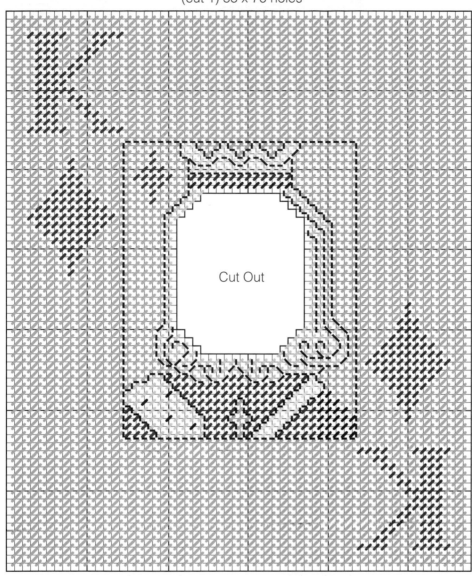

Cut Out

Holiday Photo Charms

SIZE & MATERIALS

Sizes: Angel is 3½" x 4⅝"; Snowman is 3" x 4¼"; Tree is 3¼" x 4¼"; Witch is 3" x about 9½"; Cat is 3" x about 5"; Ghost is 4½" x about 5". Each has a 1¼" x 1¼" photo window.

Materials: 1½ sheets of soft 7-count plastic canvas; Four green, four pink, two blue, two yellow and two white 7mm printed wiggle eyes; Two 3mm wiggle eyes; One purple and two lt. orange 3" lengths of 2mm plastic coils; ¼ yd. gold plaid ⅜" metallic ribbon; Craft glue or glue gun; Metallic cord (for amount see Color Key on page 20); Worsted-weight or plastic canvas yarn (for amounts see Color Key).

INSTRUCTIONS

Cutting Instructions:

(Note: Graphs on pages 20 & 23.)

A: For Angel, cut one according to graph.

B: For star, cut one according to graph.

C: For Snowman, cut one according to graph.

D: For wreath, cut one according to graph.

E: For Tree, cut one according to graph.

F: For gift, cut one according to graph.

G: For Witch, cut one according to graph.

H: For pumpkin, cut one according to graph.

I: For boots, cut two according to graph.

J: For Cat, cut one according to graph.

K: For monster, cut one according to graph.

L: For Ghost, cut one according to graph.

M: For spider, cut one according to graph.

Stitching Instructions:

1: Using colors and stitches indicated, work pieces (one I on opposite side of canvas) according to graphs; with gold cord for outer edges of Angel's halo and with matching colors as shown in photo, Overcast edges of pieces.

2: Using colors (Separate into individual plies, if desired.) and embroidery stitches indicated, embroider detail on A, C-E, G and J-M pieces as indicated on graphs.

3: Glue one photo behind cutout on B, D, F, H, K and M pieces.

4: For Angel, glue blue wiggle eyes to A; bending arms to front, glue arms to B and B to A as shown in photo.

5: For Snowman, glue yellow wiggle eyes to C; bending arms to front, glue arms to D and D to C as shown.

(Note: Cut two 2½", two ¾" and two ½" lengths of ribbon.)

6: For each bow (make 2), glue one 2½" and one ½" ribbon together according to Bow Assembly Illustration. Glue one bow to bottom of Snowman's wreath. Glue ¾" ribbons and remaining bow to F according to Gift Assembly Illustration.

7: For Tree, glue two green wiggle eyes to E; bending arms to front, glue arms to F and F to E as shown.

8: For Witch, glue two green wiggle eyes to G; bending arms to front, glue arms to H and H to G as shown.

9: Glue one I to end of one lt. orange coil, wrapping boot top extension around coil; repeat with remaining lt. orange coil and boot. Glue opposite ends of coils to back of G for legs; stretch coils to lengthen legs.

10: For Cat, glue white wiggle eyes to J and two pink wiggle eyes to K; bending arms to front, glue arms to K and K to J as shown. Glue purple coil to back for tail; stretch coil to lengthen tail, if desired.

11: For Ghost, glue two pink wiggle eyes to L and 3mm wiggle eyes to M; bending arms to front, glue arms to M and M to L as shown.

A – Angel
(cut 1) 30 x 33 holes

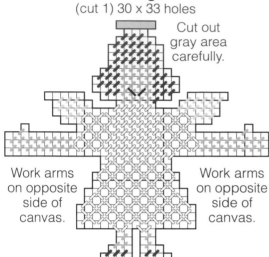

Cut out gray area carefully.

Work arms on opposite side of canvas.

Work arms on opposite side of canvas.

B – Star
(cut 1)
20 x 21 holes

Cut Out

C – Snowman
(cut 1)
28 x 31 holes

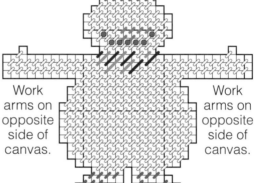

Work arms on opposite side of canvas.

Work arms on opposite side of canvas.

D – Wreath
(cut 1) 15 x 15 holes

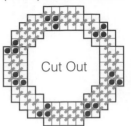

Cut Out

H – Pumpkin
(cut 1)
15 x 16 holes

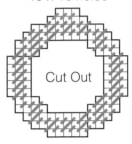

Cut Out

K – Monster
(cut 1)
16 x 18 holes

Cut Out

Bow Assembly Illustration

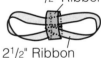

1/2" Ribbon

2 1/2" Ribbon

Gift Assembly Illustration

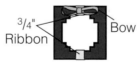

3/4" Ribbon

Bow

E – Tree
(cut 1)
28 x 31 holes

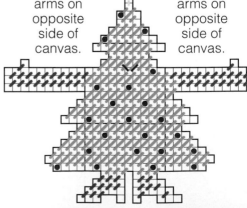

Work arms on opposite side of canvas.

Work arms on opposite side of canvas.

F – Gift
(cut 1)
13 x 13 holes

Cut Out

COLOR KEY: Holiday Photo Charms

	Metallic cord			AMOUNT
☐	Gold			8 yds.

	Worsted-weight	Nylon Plus™	Need-loft®	YARN AMOUNT
▨	White	#01	#41	24 yds.
■	Bt. Purple	–	#64	15 yds.
■	Holly	#31	#27	10 yds.
■	Black	#02	#00	9 yds.
■	Bt. Orange	#17	#58	7 yds.
■	Cinnamon	#44	#14	6 yds.
☐	Moss	#48	#25	6 yds.
■	Xmas Red	#19	#02	6 yds.
☐	Flesh Tone	–	#56	3 yds.
■	Royal	#09	#32	1 yd.

STITCH KEY:
— Backstitch/Straight Stitch
● French Knot

Apple Tissue Cover

Instructions on next page

2

Apple Tissue Cover

Photo on page 21.

SIZE & MATERIALS

Size: Snugly covers a boutique-style tissue box.

Materials: 2½ sheets of 7-count plastic canvas; Scrap of black 7-count plastic canvas; Craft glue or glue gun; Worsted-weight or plastic canvas yarn (for amounts see Color Key).

INSTRUCTIONS

Cutting Instructions:
(Note: Use black for H and clear canvas for remaining pieces.)
A: For sides, cut four according to graph.
B: For stem pieces, cut four 8 x 9 holes.
C: For leaf, cut one according to graph.
D: For worm, cut one according to graph.
E: For worm arms, cut one each according to graphs.
F: For book covers and spine, cut two 3 x 5 holes for covers and one 1 x 5 holes for spine (no spine graph).

G: For glasses, cut one according to graph.

Stitching Instructions:
(Note: Spine F and G pieces are not worked.)
1: Using colors and stitches indicated, work A-E and cover F pieces according to graphs; with fern, Overcast edges of D and E pieces.
2: Using colors (Separate into individual plies, if desired.) and embroidery stitches indicated, embroider facial detail on D as indicated on graph.
3: With red for Cover pieces and with cinnamon, Whipstitch A and B pieces together as indicated and according to Cover Assembly Illustration; with matching colors, Overcast unfinished edges.
4: For leaf, with holly, Whipstitch X edges of C right sides together as indicated; Overcast unfinished edges.
5: For book, with sail blue, Whipstitch F pieces together according to Book Assembly Illustration; Overcast unfinished edges.
6: Glue E pieces to back of D as indicated; glue book between arms and G to face as shown in photo. Glue worm and leaf to Cover as shown.🌑

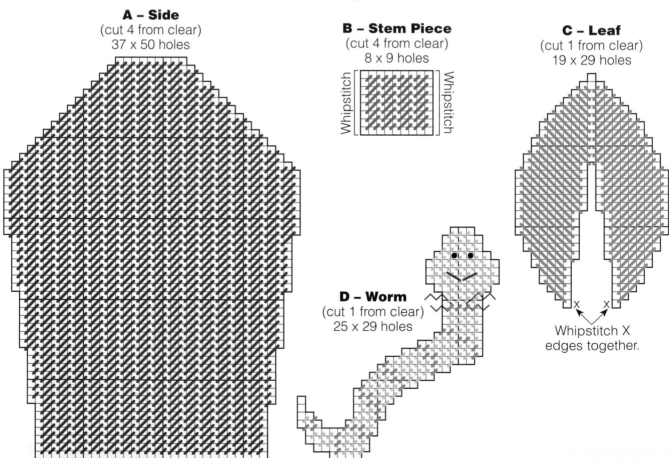

A – Side
(cut 4 from clear)
37 x 50 holes

B – Stem Piece
(cut 4 from clear)
8 x 9 holes

Whipstitch   Whipstitch

C – Leaf
(cut 1 from clear)
19 x 29 holes

D – Worm
(cut 1 from clear)
25 x 29 holes

X   X
Whipstitch X edges together.

E – Worm Arms
(cut 1 each from clear)
6 x 7 holes

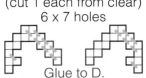

Glue to D.

F – Book Cover
(cut 2 from clear)
3 x 5 holes

G – Glasses
(cut 1 from black)
2 x 9 holes

Cut out gray
areas and around
bars carefully.

COLOR KEY: Apple Tissue Cover

Worsted-weight	Nylon Plus™	Need-loft®	YARN AMOUNT
Red	#20	#01	80 yds.
Cinnamon	#44	#14	8 yds.
Holly	#31	#27	7 yds.
Fern	#57	#23	5 yds.
Sail Blue	#04	#35	2 yds.
Black	#02	#00	¼ yd.

STITCH KEY:
— Backstitch/Straight Stitch
● French Knot
— Arm Placement

Book Assembly Illustration

Cover F

Spine F

Cover F

Cover Assembly Illustration

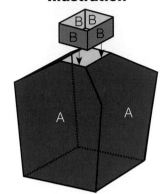

B B
B B

A   A

▣ Holiday Photo Charms

Instructions & photo on pages 18 & 19.

J – Cat
(cut 1)
27 x 31 holes

Work arms on opposite side of canvas.

Work arms on opposite side of canvas.

L – Ghost
(cut 1)
28 x 29 holes

Work arms on opposite side of canvas.

Work arms on opposite side of canvas.

I – Boot
(cut 2)
8 x 11 holes

G – Witch
(cut 1)
31 x 34 holes

Work arms on opposite side of canvas.

Work arms on opposite side of canvas.

M – Spider
(cut 1)
15 x 23 holes

Cut Out

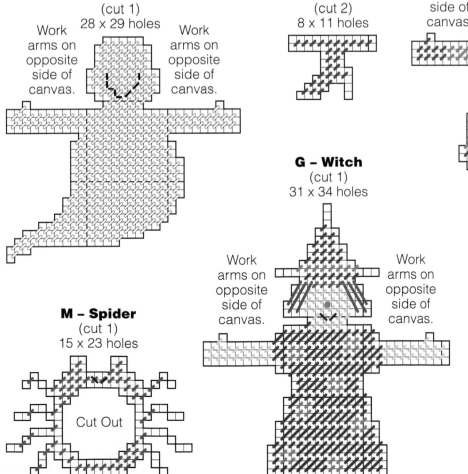

COLOR KEY: Holiday Photo Charms

Metallic cord			AMOUNT
Gold			8 yds.

Worsted-weight	Nylon Plus™	Need-loft®	YARN AMOUNT
White	#01	#41	24 yds.
Bt. Purple	–	#64	15 yds.
Holly	#31	#27	10 yds.
Black	#02	#00	9 yds.
Bt. Orange	#17	#58	7 yds.
Cinnamon	#44	#14	6 yds.
Moss	#48	#25	6 yds.
Xmas Red	#19	#02	6 yds.
Flesh Tone	–	#56	3 yds.
Royal	#09	#32	1 yd.

STITCH KEY:
— Backstitch/Straight Stitch
● French Knot

Regal Swan Box

SIZE & MATERIALS

Size: 3¾" across x 9⅛" tall.

Materials: One sheet of 7-count plastic canvas; Two 4½" plastic canvas radial circles; One clear 1-liter (33.8 fl. oz.) plastic bottle; Three rose 20mm satin ribbon roses with leaves; Seven gold metallic 12mm ribbon roses; 3" circle of aluminum foil; Six gold 3mm beads; 1 yd. white/gold ⅜" crinkle ribbon; Craft glue or glue gun; Metallic cord (for amount see Color Key); Worsted-weight or plastic canvas yarn (for amounts see Color Key).

INSTRUCTIONS

Cutting Instructions:

A: For lid side, cut one 12 x 72 holes.
B: For box side, cut one 11 x 63 holes (no graph).
C: For lid top, cut one from 4½" circle according to graph.
D: For box bottom, cut away outer four rows of holes from 4½" circle (no graph).
E: For swan sides, cut two according to graph.
F: For swan front, cut one 2 x 3 holes.
G: For crown, cut one according to graph.
H: For box bottom pull, cut one 2 x 20 holes (no graph).

Stitching Instructions:

(Note: B, D and H pieces are not worked.)
1: Using colors and stitches indicated, work A, C, E (one on opposite side of canvas), F and G pieces according to graphs. With white, Whipstitch ends of A wrong sides together as indicated on graph; using moss and Backstitch, embroider detail on A and C pieces as indicated.
2: With white, Whipstitch ends of B together; sew ends of H to D according to Box Pull Assembly Illustration. With pull facing out, Whipstitch B and D pieces together, forming box; do not Overcast unfinished edge.
3: With white, Whipstitch A and C pieces together; Overcast unfinished edge of lid.
4: With matching colors, Overcast E pieces as indicated and long edges of F; Whipstitch E and F pieces together according to Swan Assembly Dia-

gram; glue 3mm beads to each swan side as indicated.
5: With gold cord, Whipstitch Y edges and ends of G wrong sides together as indicated; Overcast unfinished edges.
6: Cut away bottom of plastic bottle according to Bottle Cutting Illustration. Remove label; if label glue remains, remove with baby oil. Wash with hot water and soap and dry bottle. Cover cap with foil; secure cap on bottle top and glue in place.
7: Glue pieces together according to Regal Swan Box Assembly Diagram.◉

E – Swan Side
(cut 2)
14 x 16 holes

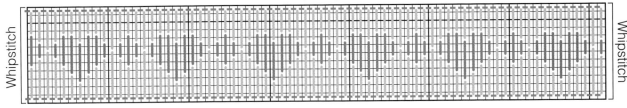

Overcast between arrows.

Whipstitch

Whipstitch to F.

Whipstitch

F – Swan Front
(cut 1)
2 x 3 holes

Whipstitch to one E.

Whipstitch to one E.

COLOR KEY: Regal Swan Box

Metallic cord			AMOUNT
Gold			14 yds.

Worsted-weight	Nylon Plus™	Need-loft®	YARN AMOUNT
White	#01	#41	20 yds.
Lavender	#12	#05	14 yds.
Moss	#48	#25	5 yds.

STITCH KEY:
— Backstitch/Straight Stitch
○ Bead Placement

A – Lid Side (cut 1) 12 x 72 holes

Whipstitch

Whipstitch

G – Crown
(cut 1) 12 x 35 holes

Whipstitch

Whipstitch

Y Y Y Y Y Y Y Y Y Y

Whipstitch Y edges together.

Swan Assembly Diagram

Step 2: Whipstitch F and E pieces together.

Step 1: Whipstitch head and tail areas together.

E

E

F

Bottle Cutting Illustration

11"

Bottle

Cut

Box Pull Assembly Illustration
(bottom view)

Stitch

H

D

Stitch

C – Lid Top
(cut 1 from 4½" circle)
Cut away gray areas.

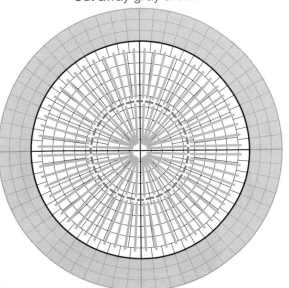

Regal Swan Box Assembly Diagram

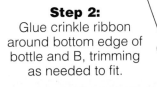

Step 1: Glue swan to C and one 20mm ribbon rose to C on each side of swan; glue bottom edge of bottle to C.

Gold Ribbon Rose

Swan

Crinkle Ribbon

Step 2: Glue crinkle ribbon around bottom edge of bottle and B, trimming as needed to fit.

G

Bottle

20mm Ribbon Rose

C

A

B

Step 3: Glue G to bottle neck and one gold ribbon rose below each point of crown.

Step 4: Glue remaining 20mm ribbon rose to bottle lid top.

CHAPTER 2

Glenda Chamberlain

Photograph by Russ Chaffin, *The Needlecraft Shop* Staff Photographer

Designer Glenda Chamberlain comes from a long line of artisans. Her family settled in East Texas before the Civil War, when the creative arts were vital to the quality of life. Glenda recalls that both of her grandmothers expressed their talents in quilt-making, macrame, ceramics and lace making. Each of Glenda's teenage boys, Kyle and Cory, are showing similar creative traits with plastic canvas.

In addition to designing, Glenda's career in publishing has been quite varied. Now production coordinator for *The Needlecraft Shop*, Glenda has served in numerous capacities since coming on staff in 1992. She has been a production manager, editor and art director, and prior to 1992 owned and published a weekly advertiser that served her area for nine years.

Her first plastic canvas design was published in 1993, and Glenda attributes the motivation to try her hand at designing to working around other talented and creative people.

Glenda and her husband of 24 years, Robert, make their home in the same rural community in Texas where she grew up. "I think a close family, small towns and friends you've always known are the greatest joys in life," says Glenda.

Floral Memories

SIZE & MATERIALS

Sizes: Frame is 7⅝" x 11⅜" with two 3" x 5" photo windows; Trinket Box is 4⅝" square x 2⅛" tall. Measurements do not include flowers.

Materials: Six sheets of 7-count plastic canvas; Craft glue or glue gun; Worsted-weight or plastic canvas yarn (for amounts see Color Key).

INSTRUCTIONS

Cutting Instructions:

(Note: Graphs continued on page 30.)

A: For Frame fronts, cut two according to graph.

B: For Frame mats, cut two according to graph.

C: For Frame backings, cut two 35 x 50 holes (no graph).

D: For Trinket Box lid top, cut one 29 x 29 holes.

E: For Trinket Box lid sides, cut four 4 x 29 holes.

F: For Trinket Box bottom, cut one 27 x 27 holes (no graph).

G: For Trinket Box sides, cut four 12 x 27 holes.

H: For leaves, cut eight according to graph.

I: For flower petals, cut thirty-six according to graph.

J: For flower centers, cut six according to graph.

Stitching Instructions:

(Note: C and F pieces are not worked.)

1: Using colors and stitches indicated, work A, B (leave uncoded area unworked), D, E and G-J pieces according to graphs. With aqua for fronts and white for mats, Overcast cutout edges of A and B pieces; with matching colors, Overcast edges of H-J pieces.

2: With aqua, Whipstitch A-C pieces together according to Frame Assembly Diagram on page 30; Whipstitch D-G pieces together according to Box Assembly Illustration. Overcast unfinished edges of box and lid.

3: For each flower; glue six I and one J together according to Flower Assembly Illustration on page 30. Glue flowers and leaves to Frame and Trinket Box lid as desired or as shown in photo.⊛

G – Trinket Box Side
(cut 4) 12 x 27 holes

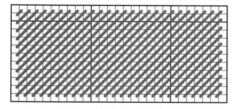

D – Trinket Box Lid Top
(cut 1) 29 x 29 holes

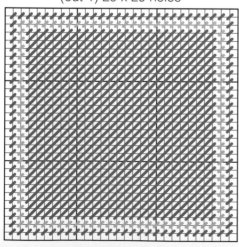

COLOR KEY: Floral Memories

	Worsted-weight	Nylon Plus™	Need-loft®	YARN AMOUNT
■	Aqua	#60	#51	50 yds.
▨	White	#01	#41	14 yds.
■	Plum	#55	#59	12 yds.
▨	Aqua Light	#39	#49	10 yds.
▨	Forest	#32	#29	10 yds.
▨	Straw	#41	#19	2 yds.

STITCH KEY:
— Backstitch/Straight Stitch

Box Assembly Illustration

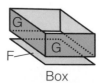

Lid

Box

Floral Memories

Instructions & photo on pages 28 & 29.

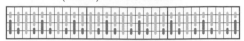

A – Frame Front
(cut 2) 37 x 50 holes

Cut Out

H – Leaf
(cut 8)
7 x 11 holes

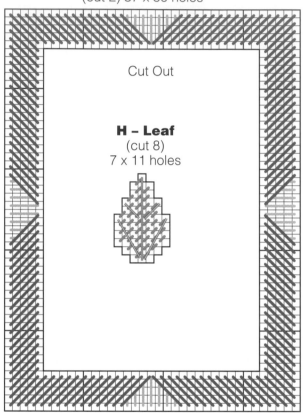

B – Frame Mat
(cut 2) 37 x 50 holes

Cut Out

I – Flower Petal
(cut 36)
5 x 5 holes

Carefully cut
through bars.

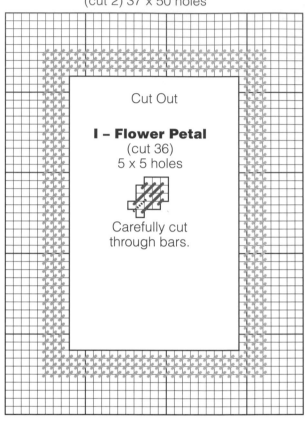

J – Flower Center
(cut 6)
3 x 3 holes

**Flower Assembly
Illustration**

Frame Assembly Diagram

Step 1:
(front view)
Holding right side of one B to
wrong side of each A,
Whipstitch together at one long
edge through all thicknesses.

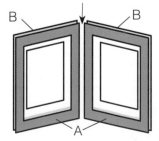

Step 2:
(back view)
Whipstitch one C to
outer edges on each
side of assembly.

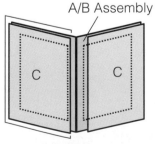

A/B Assembly

Step 3:
Whipstitch unfinished edges
of A/B assembly together.

COLOR KEY: Floral Memories

Worsted-weight	Nylon Plus™	Need-loft®	YARN AMOUNT
Aqua	#60	#51	50 yds.
White	#01	#41	14 yds.
Plum	#55	#59	12 yds.
Aqua Light	#39	#49	10 yds.
Forest	#32	#29	10 yds.
Straw	#41	#19	2 yds.

STITCH KEY:
— Backstitch/Straight Stitch

Tumbling Baskets Tote

Instructions on next page

◼ Tumbling Baskets Tote

Photo on page 31.

SIZE & MATERIALS

Size: 3" x 12⅜" x 12⅜" tall, not including handles.

Materials: Three 12" x 18" or larger sheets of 7-count plastic canvas; Craft glue or glue gun; Worsted-weight or plastic canvas yarn (for amounts see Color Key).

INSTRUCTIONS

Cutting Instructions:
A: For sides, cut two 81 x 81 holes.
B: For ends, cut two 19 x 81 holes.
C: For bottom, cut one 19 x 81 holes (no graph).
D: For handles, cut two 6 x 89 holes.
E: For baskets, cut eight according to graph.
F: For basket handles, cut eight according to graph.

B – End
(cut 2) 19 x 81 holes

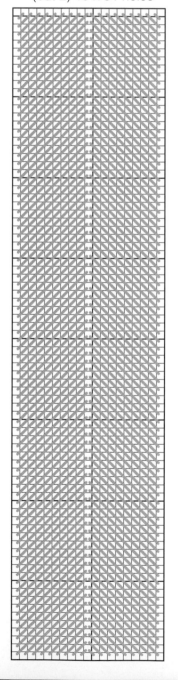

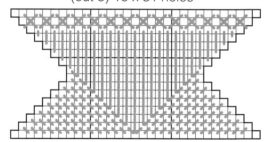

COLOR KEY: Tumbling Baskets Tote

	Worsted-weight	Nylon Plus™	Need-loft®	YARN AMOUNT
	White	#01	#41	3½ oz.
	Baby Green	#28	#26	22 yds.
	Lilac	#22	#45	22 yds.
	Peach	#46	#47	22 yds.
	Sail Blue	#04	#35	22 yds.

STITCH KEY:
☐ Basket Placement
☐ Basket Handle Placement

E – Basket
(cut 8) 16 x 31 holes

F – Basket Handle
(cut 8) 15 x 25 holes

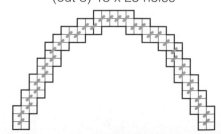

Stitching Instructions:

(Note: C piece is not worked.)

1: Using colors and stitches indicated, work A, B, D, two E and two F pieces according to graphs; substituting sail blue, peach and baby green for lilac, work two of each remaining E and F pieces in each color according to graphs. With matching colors, Overcast edges of E and F pieces; with white, Overcast long edges of D pieces.

2: With white, Whipstitch A-D pieces together; Overcast unfinished edges, catching ends of one D to each side as indicated on graph as you work.

3: Glue one of each color basket and handle to each side as indicated (see photo). ⊛

Handle Attachment

Handle Attachment

A – Side
(cut 2) 81 x 81 holes

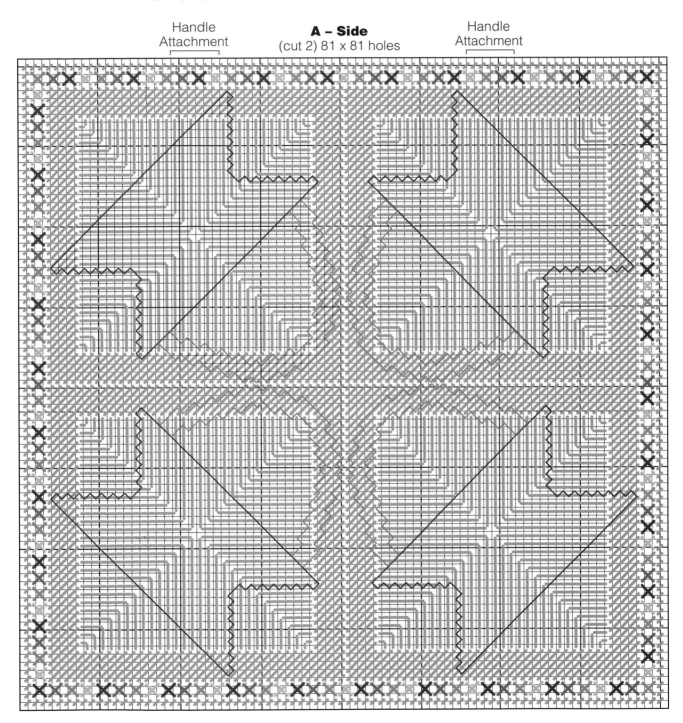

D – Handle (cut 2) 6 x 89 holes

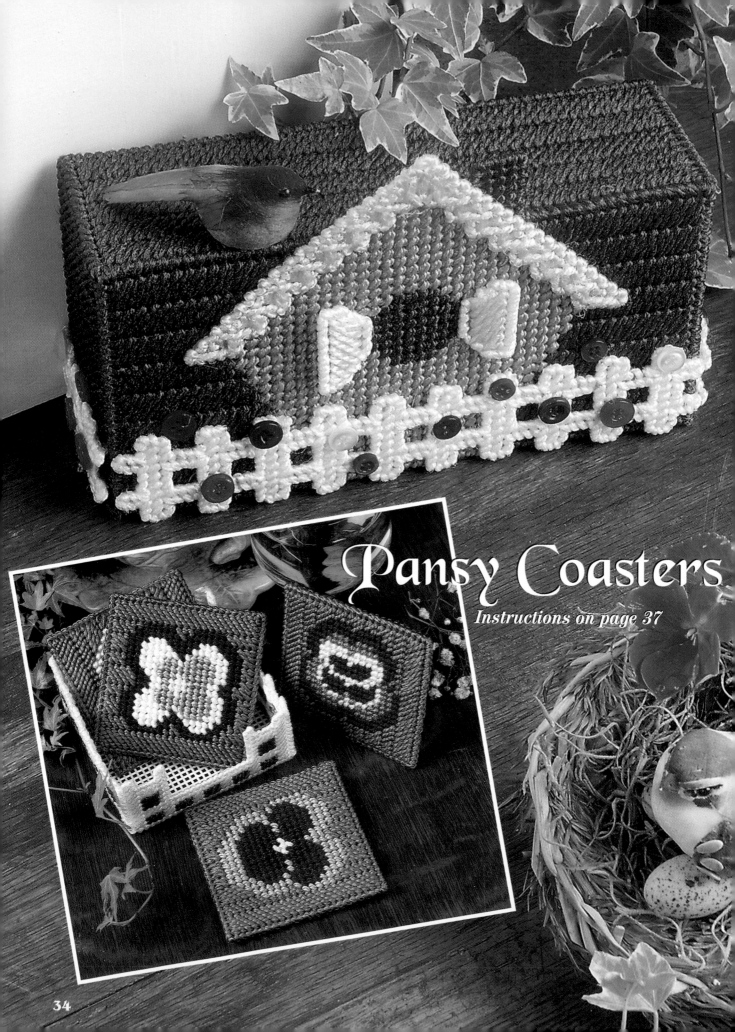

Pansy Coasters

Instructions on page 37

Birdhouse Doorstop

SIZE & MATERIALS

Size: 2½" x 8⅛" x 5½" tall.

Materials: Two sheets of 7-count plastic canvas; brick to fit above dimensions or a zip-close bag filled with sand, gravel or other weighting material; 19 small assorted sizes and colors of decorative buttons; Small artificial bird; Craft glue or glue gun; Worsted-weight or plastic canvas yarn (for amounts see Color Key).

INSTRUCTIONS

Cutting Instructions:
(Note: Graphs continued on page 36.)
A: For front, cut one according to graph.
B: For back, cut one 26 x 51 holes.
C: For top and bottom, cut two (one for top and one for bottom) 16 x 51 holes (no bottom graph).

D: For ends, cut two 16 x 26 holes.
E: For fence front, cut one according to graph.
F: For fence sides, cut two according to graph.
G: For roof, cut one according to graph.
H: For shutter #1, cut one according to graph.
I: For shutter #2, cut one according to graph.

Stitching Instructions:
(Note: One C is not worked for bottom.)
1: Using colors and stitches indicated, work A, B, one C for top and D-I pieces according to graphs; with white for shutters and with matching colors, Overcast edges of E-I pieces.
2: With forest, Whipstitch A-D pieces together according to Doorstop Assembly Illustration on page 36, inserting weight before closing; with matching colors, Overcast unfinished edges.
3: Glue roof to Doorstop as indicated on graph; glue fences, shutters, buttons and bird to Doorstop as shown in photo.

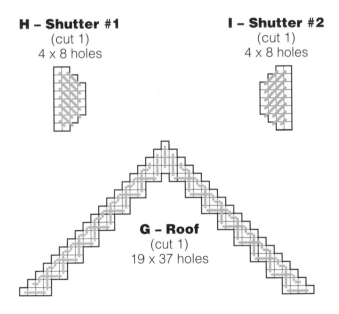

H – Shutter #1
(cut 1)
4 x 8 holes

I – Shutter #2
(cut 1)
4 x 8 holes

G – Roof
(cut 1)
19 x 37 holes

COLOR KEY: Birdhouse Doorstop

	Worsted-weight	Nylon Plus™	Need-loft®	YARN AMOUNT
	Forest	#32	#29	58 yds.
	Bt. Blue	–	#60	11 yds.
	White	#01	#41	10 yds.
	Straw	#41	#19	7 yds.
	Cinnamon	#44	#14	2 yds.

STITCH KEY:
☐ Roof Placement

Birdhouse Doorstop

Instructions & photo on pages 34 & 35.

A – Front
(cut 1)
34 x 51 holes

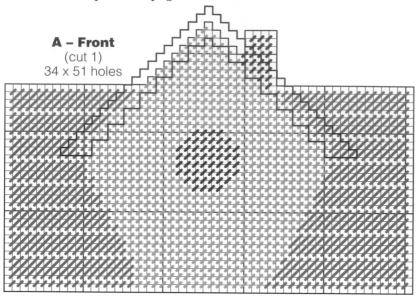

B – Back
(cut 1) 26 x 51 holes

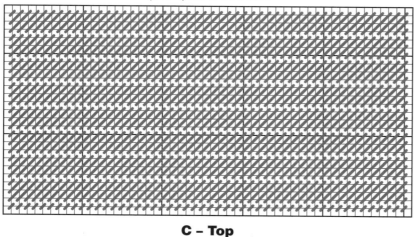

C – Top
(cut 1) 16 x 51 holes

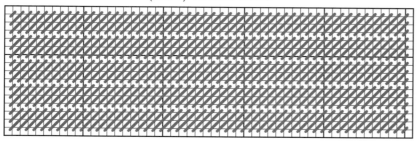

E – Fence Front
(cut 1) 9 x 51 holes

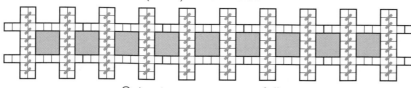

Cut out gray areas carefully.

COLOR KEY: Birdhouse Doorstop

	Worsted-weight	Nylon Plus™	Need-loft®	YARN AMOUNT
■	Forest	#32	#29	58 yds.
■	Bt. Blue	–	#60	11 yds.
■	White	#01	#41	10 yds.
■	Straw	#41	#19	7 yds.
■	Cinnamon	#44	#14	2 yds.

STITCH KEY:

☐ Roof Placement

D – End
(cut 2) 16 x 26 holes

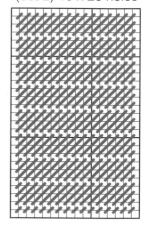

F – Fence Side
(cut 2) 9 x 16 holes

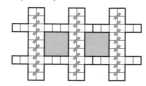

Cut out gray areas carefully.

Doorstop Assembly Illustration

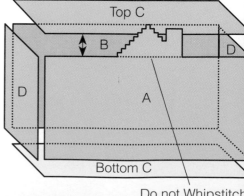

Top C

B

D

D

A

Bottom C

Do not Whipstitch.

Pansy Coasters

Photo on page 34.

SIZE & MATERIALS

Sizes: Holder is 4⅜" square x 1⅞" tall; each Coaster is 3⅝" square.

Materials: 1½ sheets of clear 7-count plastic canvas; One sheet of white 7-count plastic canvas; Worsted-weight or plastic canvas yarn (for amounts see Color Key).

INSTRUCTIONS

Cutting Instructions:
(Note: Graphs continued on page 38.)

A: For Holder front, cut one from clear according to graph.

B: For Holder sides and back, cut three (two for sides and one for back) from clear according to graph.

C: For Holder bottom, cut one from white 28 x 28 holes (no graph).

D: For Coasters #1–#4 fronts and backings, cut eight (four from clear for fronts and four from white for backings) 24 x 24 holes (no backing graphs).

Stitching Instructions:
(Note: C and backing D pieces are not worked.)

1: Using colors and stitches indicated, work A, B and front D pieces according to graphs.

2: With white, Whipstitch A-C pieces together according to Holder Assembly Illustration; Overcast unfinished edges.

3: For each Coaster, holding one backing D to wrong side of one front D, with holly, Whipstitch together. ❀

A – Holder Front
(cut 1 from clear) 12 x 28 holes

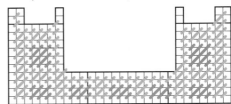

B – Holder Side & Back
(cut 3 from clear) 12 x 28 holes

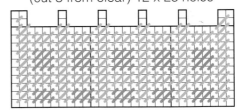

Holder Assembly Illustration

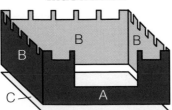

COLOR KEY: Pansy Coasters

	Worsted-weight	Nylon Plus™	Need-loft®	YARN AMOUNT
	Holly	#31	#27	24 yds.
	White	#01	#41	10 yds.
	Purple	#21	#46	5 yds.
	Baby Yellow	#42	#21	2 yds.
	Lilac	#22	#45	2 yds.
	Straw	#41	#19	2 yds.
	Black	#02	#00	1 yd.
	Lavender	#12	#05	1 yd.

Pansy Coasters

Instructions & photo on page 37.

D – Coaster #2 Front
(cut 1 from clear) 24 x 24 holes

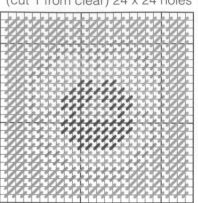

D – Coaster #1 Front
(cut 1 from clear) 24 x 24 holes

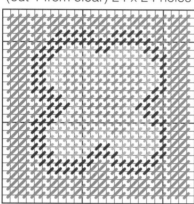

D – Coaster #3 Front
(cut 1 from clear) 24 x 24 holes

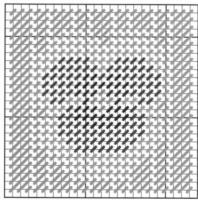

D – Coaster #4 Front
(cut 1 from clear) 24 x 24 holes

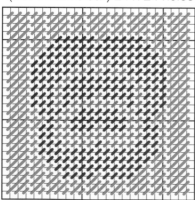

COLOR KEY: Pansy Coasters

	Worsted-weight	Nylon Plus™	Need-loft®	YARN AMOUNT
	Holly	#31	#27	24 yds.
	White	#01	#41	10 yds.
	Purple	#21	#46	5 yds.
	Baby Yellow	#42	#21	2 yds.
	Lilac	#22	#45	2 yds.
	Straw	#41	#19	2 yds.
	Black	#02	#00	1 yd.
	Lavender	#12	#05	1 yd.

Reflections of Calvary

Size: 3" x 6½" x 10½" tall; holds two 2½"-across x 2⅝"-tall glass candle holders.

Materials: Four sheets of 7-count plastic canvas; Craft glue or glue gun; Metallic cord (for amount see Color Key on page 40); Worsted-weight or plastic canvas yarn (for amounts see Color Key).

INSTRUCTIONS

Cutting Instructions:
(Note: Graphs on page 40.)
A: For Holder window and backings, cut three (one for window and two for backings) according to graph.
B: For Holder front, cut one according to graph.
C: For Holder bottom, cut one according to graph.
D: For cross, cut one according to graph.

Stitching Instructions:
(Note: Two A pieces and C are not worked.)
1: Using colors and stitches indicated, work one A for window, B and D pieces according to graphs; with gold, Overcast edges of D.
2: With royal dark, Whipstitch A-C pieces together as indicated on graphs and according to Holder Assembly Diagram.
3: Glue cross to Holder window as shown in photo.◉

Reflections of Calvary

Instructions & photo on page 39.

COLOR KEY: Reflections of Calvary

Metallic cord			AMOUNT
Gold			14 yds.

Worsted-weight	Nylon Plus™	Need-loft®	YARN AMOUNT
Royal Dark	#07	#48	36 yds.
Xmas Green	#58	#28	8 yds.
Watermelon	#54	#55	7 yds.
Bt. Purple	–	#64	5 yds.

A – Holder Window & Backing
(cut 3) 39 x 68 holes

C – Holder Bottom
(cut 1) 18 x 39 holes

D – Cross
(cut 1)
43 x 56 holes

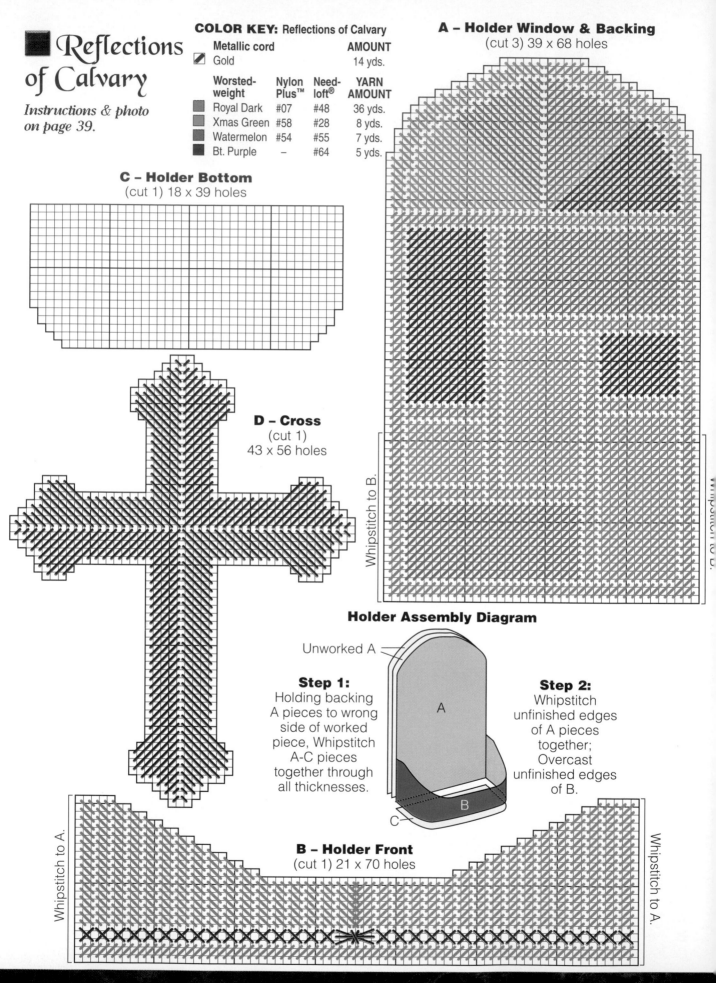

Whipstitch to B.

Holder Assembly Diagram

Unworked A

Step 1:
Holding backing A pieces to wrong side of worked piece, Whipstitch A-C pieces together through all thicknesses.

Step 2:
Whipstitch unfinished edges of A pieces together; Overcast unfinished edges of B.

A

B

C

B – Holder Front
(cut 1) 21 x 70 holes

Whipstitch to A.

Whipstitch to A.

Tissue Books

SIZE & MATERIALS

Size: 5¾" x 10¼" x 3⅝" tall, and holds a 3" x 9" x 4¾" tissue box.

Materials: Two sheets of 7-count plastic canvas; Medium metallic braid or metallic cord (for amounts see Color Key on page 43); Worsted-weight or plastic canvas yarn (for amounts see Color Key).

INSTRUCTIONS

Cutting Instructions:
(Note: Graphs on pages 42-43.)
A: For top, cut one according to graph.
B: For sides #1 and #2, cut one each 23 x 66 holes.
C: For ends, cut two 23 x 34 holes.
D: For spine #1, cut one 8 x 66 holes.
E: For spine #2, cut one 9 x 66 holes.
F: For spine #3, cut one 10 x 66 holes.

Stitching Instructions:
(Note: B#2 is not worked.)
1: Using colors and stitches indicated, work B#1 and C pieces according to graphs. Using aqua for top and spine #1, purple for spine #2, burgundy for spine #3 and Continental Stitch, work A and D-F pieces. With matching colors, Overcast cutout edges of A and short ends of D-F pieces.
2: Using metallic ribbon or braid in colors and embroidery stitches indicated, embroider detail on A and D-F pieces as indicated on graphs.
3: With matching colors, Whipstitch pieces together as indicated and according to Cover Assembly Diagram on page 43.◉

■ Tissue Books

Instructions & photo on page 41.

A – Top
(cut 1) 34 x 66 holes

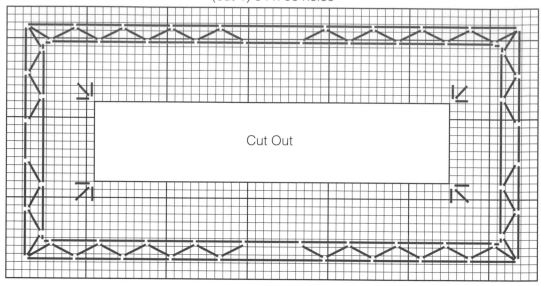

Cut Out

D – Spine #1
(cut 1) 8 x 66 holes

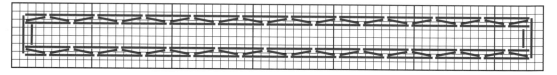

E – Spine #2
(cut 1) 9 x 66 holes

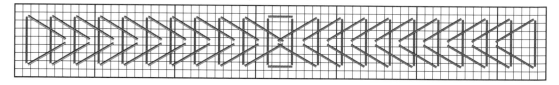

F – Spine #3
(cut 1) 10 x 66 holes

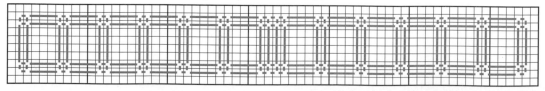

B – Side #1
(cut 1) 23 x 66 holes

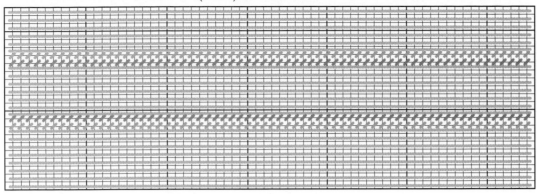

B – Side #2
(cut 1) 23 x 66 holes

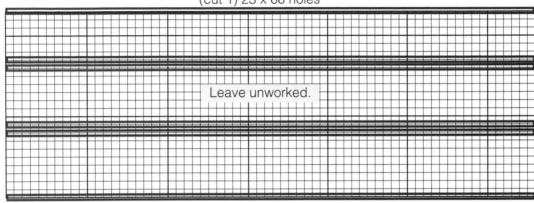

Leave unworked.

C – End
(cut 2) 23 x 34 holes

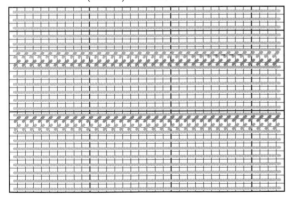

COLOR KEY: Tissue Books

Med. metallic braid or cord			AMOUNT
Gold			18 yds.
Pink			9 yds.
Silver			6 yds.

Worsted-weight	Nylon Plus™	Need-loft®	YARN AMOUNT
Teal Blue	#08	#50	41 yds.
Burgundy	#13	#03	20 yds.
Sandstone	#47	#16	26 yds.
Purple	#21	#46	15 yds.

STITCH KEY:
- Backstitch/Straight Stitch
- ☐ Spine #1 Attachment
- ☐ Spine #2 Attachment
- ☐ Spine #3 Attachment

Cover Assembly Diagram
(Pieces are shown in different colors for contrast.)

Step 1:
With teal blue, Whipstitch one long edge of D to one long edge of A and to unworked B#2 through all thicknesses; Whipstitch opposite long edge of D to unworked B#2 (D will bow outward).

Step 2:
With matching colors, Whipstitch long edges of E and F pieces to B#2.

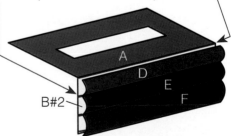

Step 3:
With teal blue for top and with matching colors, Whipstitch A-C pieces together.

Step 4:
With burgundy, Overcast unfinished bottom edges.

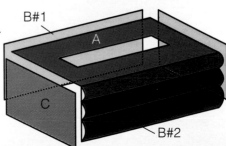

CHAPTER 3

Diane T. Ray

Photograph by Gary O. Scott, Hobbs, New Mexico

Designer Diane T. Ray creates a seemingly endless stream of practical and unique design ideas. Beyond their pleasing overall appearance, Diane's projects are very well known as reflections of her minute attention to each and every detail. Her designs incorporate her talents as architect, builder, color coordinator and researcher. Many hours are spent pouring over encyclopedias and how-to books before her ideas even reach the sketch stage. Known for her realism and practicality, Diane transforms ordinary household items into spiffy, plastic canvas originals that hold up to hands-on use.

Just after sunup on June 20, 1998, Diane became a grandmother for the first time. Her new grandson, Brice Lee, who weighed in at six pounds, 11 ounces, arrived just in time for Father's Day. Diane's son, Todd, and his wife, Michelle, are the proud parents.

Diane and her husband, Rick, enjoy traveling and plan to travel even more extensively when he retires in a few years. When she is not stitching or enjoying her new grandson, Diane works on her computer or in her flower garden.

Victorian Vanity Set

SIZE & MATERIALS

Sizes: Pitcher is 4¾" x 8" x 9¾" tall; Bowl is 9¼" across x 2⅛" tall; Jewelry Holder is 5" across x 2⅜" tall.

Materials: 3½ sheets of clear and 1½ sheets of pink 7-count plastic canvas; Craft glue or glue gun; Metallic cord (for amount see Color Key on page 48); Six-strand embroidery floss (for amount see Color Key); Worsted-weight or plastic canvas yarn (for amounts see Color Key).

INSTRUCTIONS

Cutting Instructions:
(Note: Graphs on pages 48-50.)
A: For Pitcher sides #1, cut one each from clear according to graphs.
B: For Pitcher sides #2, cut one each from clear according to graphs.
C: For Pitcher sides #3, cut one each from clear according to graphs.
D: For Pitcher bottom, cut one from clear according to graph.
E: For Pitcher handle, cut one from clear according to graph.
F: For Bowl motif sides, cut two from clear according to graph.
G: For Bowl solid sides, cut four from clear according to graph.
H: For Bowl bottom and bottom lining, cut two (one from clear for bottom and one from pink for bottom lining) according to graph.
I: For Bowl side linings, cut six from pink according to graph.
J: For Bowl rim pieces, cut six from clear according to graph.
K: For Jewelry Holder sides, cut six from clear according to graph.
L: For Jewelry Holder bottom, cut one from clear

according to graph.
M: For Jewelry Holder ring stand sides, cut four from clear according to graph.
N: For Jewelry Holder ring stand top, cut one from clear 1 x 1 hole (no graph).

Stitching Instructions:
(Note: D, H and I pieces are not worked.)
1: Using colors (Separate orchid into individual plies for flower petals, if desired.) and stitches indicated, work A-C, E-G and J-M pieces according to graphs; fill in uncoded areas of A-C, F and L (leave indicated area of L unworked) pieces using baby blue and Continental Stitch. With cord, Overcast edges of E.
2: Using orchid (Separate into individual plies, if desired.) and French Knot, embroider flower centers on A-C, F and L pieces as indicated on graphs; using six strands floss and Backstitch, embroider stems as indicated.
3: Whipstitch and assemble A-E pieces as indicated and according to Pitcher Assembly Diagram on page 50.
4: Whipstitch and assemble F-J pieces as indicated and according to Bowl Assembly Diagram on page 49.
5: Whipstitch and assemble K-N pieces as indicated and according to Jewelry Holder Assembly Diagram.✸

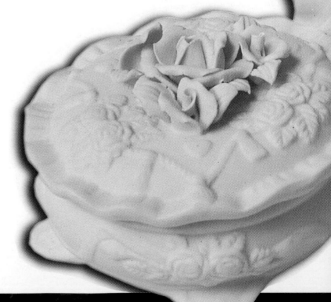

Complement your vanity with the artistic flair of an antique boudoir set.

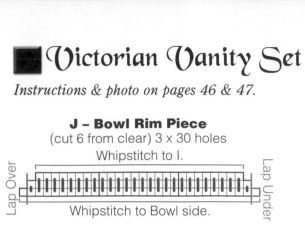

Victorian Vanity Set

Instructions & photo on pages 46 & 47.

H – Bowl Bottom & Bottom Lining
(cut 1 from each color) 41 x 50 holes

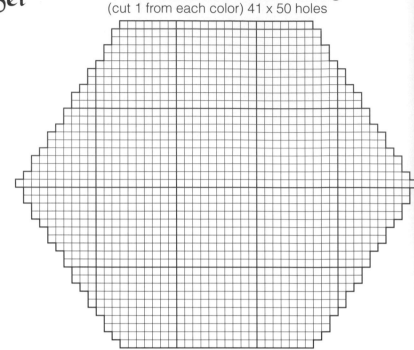

J – Bowl Rim Piece
(cut 6 from clear) 3 x 30 holes

Whipstitch to I.

Lap Over

Lap Under

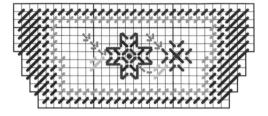

Whipstitch to Bowl side.

F – Bowl Motif Side
(cut 2 from clear) 13 x 30 holes

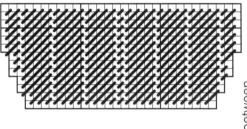

G – Bowl Solid Side
(cut 4 from clear) 13 x 30 holes

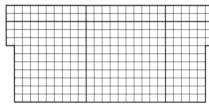

I – Bowl Side Lining
(cut 6 from pink) 12 x 26 holes

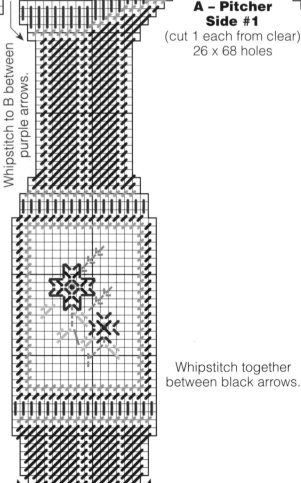

A – Pitcher Side #1
(cut 1 each from clear) 26 x 68 holes

Whipstitch to B between purple arrows.

purple arrows.

Whipstitch together between black arrows.

COLOR KEY: Victorian Vanity Set

	Metallic cord			AMOUNT
▨	White/Silver			30 yds.
	Embroidery floss			**AMOUNT**
▨	Dk. Green			6 yds.

	Worsted-weight	Nylon Plus™	Need-loft®	YARN AMOUNT
■	Violet	#49	#04	68 yds.
□	Baby Blue	#05	#36	30 yds.
■	Orchid	#56	#44	24 yds.
▨	Mint	#30	#24	6 yds.

STITCH KEY:
— Backstitch/Straight Stitch
● French Knot
☐ Unworked Area/Ring Stand Attachment

Bowl Assembly Diagram
(Some pieces are shown in different colors for contrast.)

Step 1:
With violet, Whipstitch F, G and bottom
H pieces together, forming Bowl.

Step 3:
With orchid, Whipstitch side edges
of I pieces together, forming lining
assembly.

Step 2:
Set bottom
lining H
inside
assembly;
lining is not
attached.

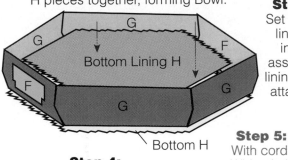
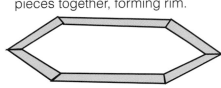

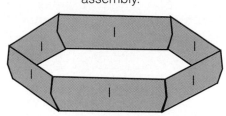
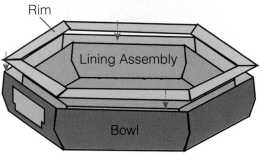

Step 4:
Overlapping bottom holes,
Whipstitch side edges of J
pieces together, forming rim.

Step 5:
With cord,
Whipstitch
Bowl, lining
assembly and
rim together.
(NOTE:
Bottom edges
of lining
assembly are
not attached.)

Rim

Lining Assembly

Bowl

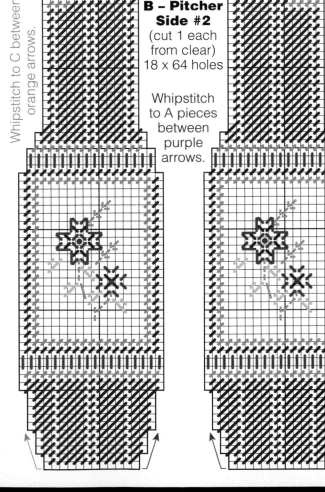

Whipstitch to C between orange arrows.

B – Pitcher Side #2
(cut 1 each
from clear)
18 x 64 holes

Whipstitch
to A pieces
between
purple
arrows.

Whipstitch to C between orange arrows.

K – Jewelry Holder Side
(cut 6 from clear)
8 x 15 holes

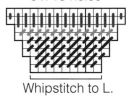

Whipstitch to L.

**M – Jewlery
Holder Ring
Stand Side**
(cut 4 from clear)
3 x 13 holes

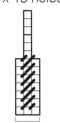

Whipstitch
to L.

L – Jewelry Holder Bottom
(cut 1 from clear) 15 x 17 holes

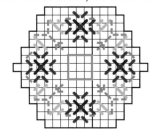

D – Pitcher Bottom
(cut 1 from clear) 21 x 24 holes

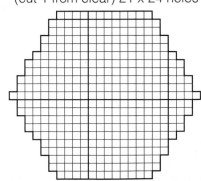

Victorian Vanity Set

Instructions & photo on pages 46 & 47.

Pitcher Assembly Diagram

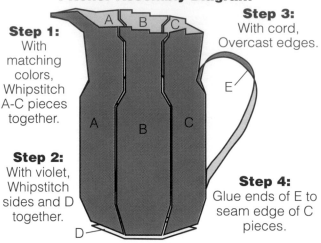

Step 1:
With matching colors, Whipstitch A-C pieces together.

Step 2:
With violet, Whipstitch sides and D together.

Step 3:
With cord, Overcast edges.

Step 4:
Glue ends of E to seam edge of C pieces.

Jewelry Holder Assembly Diagram
(Some pieces are shown in different colors for contrast.)

Step 1:
With matching colors, Whipstitch side edges of K pieces right sides together.

Step 2:
With cord, Whipstitch M and N pieces together, forming ring stand; Whipstitch stand to right side of L.

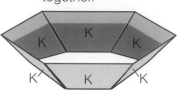

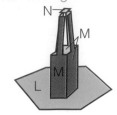

Step 3:
Whipstitch sides and L together; Overcast unfinished edges.

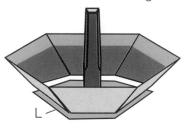

E – Pitcher Handle
(cut 1 from clear)
5 x 60 holes

Bend downward and glue right side to neck of Pitcher.

Glue wrong side over seam at lower border of motif.

COLOR KEY: Victorian Vanity Set

	Metallic cord			AMOUNT
	White/Silver			30 yds.

	Embroidery floss			AMOUNT
	Dk. Green			6 yds.

	Worsted-weight	Nylon Plus™	Need-loft®	YARN AMOUNT
	Violet	#49	#04	68 yds.
	Baby Blue	#05	#36	30 yds.
	Orchid	#56	#44	24 yds.
	Mint	#30	#24	6 yds.

STITCH KEY:
— Backstitch/Straight Stitch
• French Knot
☐ Unworked Area/Ring Stand Attachment

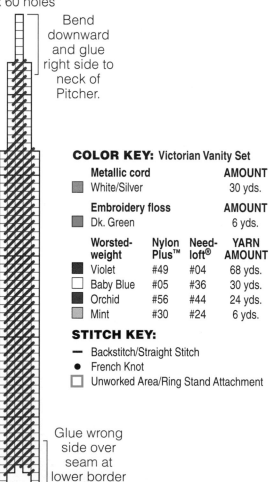

Whipstitch to B between orange arrows.

C – Pitcher Side #3
(cut 1 each from clear)
18 x 62 holes

Whipstitch to together between black arrows.

Whipstitch to B between orange arrows.

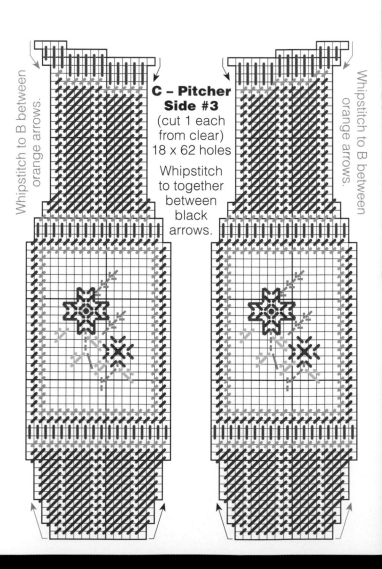

Desert Jewels

Instructions on next page

■Desert Jewels

Photo on page 51.

SIZE & MATERIALS

Sizes: Tissue Cover loosely covers a boutique-style tissue box; Pot is 4¾" square x 5⅛" tall; Switch Cover is 3" x 4¾".

Materials: Three sheets of 7-count plastic canvas; Two antique dk. turquoise 12mm Athenian beads; One dk. lilac 8mm pony bead; 20" silver 4mm bead strand; Two 1" square pieces of double-sided mounting tape; Velcro® closure (optional); Craft glue or glue gun; Metallic cord (for amounts see Color Key); Worsted-weight or plastic canvas yarn (for amounts see Color Key).

INSTRUCTIONS

Cutting Instructions:

A: For Tissue Cover top, cut one according to graph.

B: For Tissue Cover sides, cut four 31 x 37 holes.

C: For Tissue Cover optional bottom and flap, cut one 31 x 31 holes for bottom and one 12 x 31 holes for flap.

D: For Pot sides, cut four according to graph.

E: For Pot lips, cut four 5 x 23 holes.

F: For Pot bottom, cut one 21 x 21 holes (no graph).

G: For Switch Cover, cut one according to graph.

Stitching Instructions:

(Note: C and F pieces are not worked.)

1: Using colors and stitches indicated, work A, B, D, E and G pieces according to graphs. With turquoise, Overcast edges of G and cutout edges of A.

2: Using aqua/silver cord and Backstitch, embroider motif center detail on B and D pieces as indicated on graphs.

3: For Switch Cover, secure G to single switch plate with double-sided tape.

4: For Tissue Cover, with turquoise, Whipstitch A and B pieces together. For optional bottom, Whipstitch C pieces together and to one side according to Optional Cover Bottom Assembly Illustration; Overcast unfinished edges of Cover. If desired, glue closure to flap and inside of Cover.

5: For Pot, Whipstitch and assemble D-F pieces and beads as indicated and according to Pot Assembly Diagram.❂

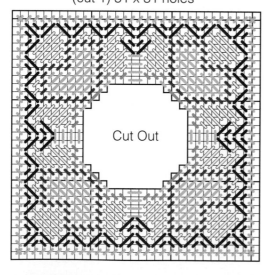

A – Tissue Cover Top
(cut 1) 31 x 31 holes

Cut Out

B – Tissue Cover Side
(cut 4) 31 x 37 holes

COLOR KEY: Desert Jewels

	Metallic cord			AMOUNT
■	Lavender/Silver			18 yds.
▨	Aqua/Silver			12 yds.

	Worsted-weight	Red Heart Jewel Tones®	Nylon Plus™	YARN AMOUNT
▨	Turquoise	#3388	–	40 yds.
▨	White	–	#01	35 yds.
■	Brilliant	#3059	–	30 yds.

STITCH KEY:

— Backstitch/Straight Stitch

E – Pot Lip
(cut 4) 5 x 23 holes

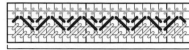

Whipstitch to D.

D – Pot Side
(cut 4) 30 x 31 holes
Whipstitch to E.

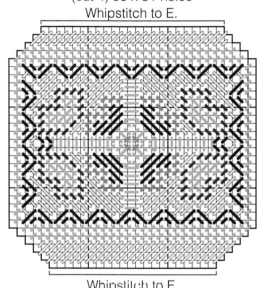

Whipstitch to F.

Optional Cover Bottom Assembly Illustration

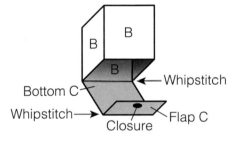

Bottom C

Whipstitch

Closure

Whipstitch

Flap C

G – Switch Cover
(cut 1) 19 x 31 holes

Cut Out

Pot Assembly Diagram
(Pieces are shown in different colors for contrast.)

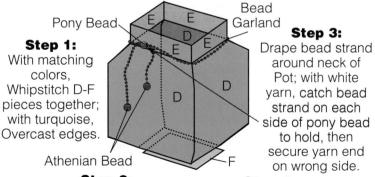

Pony Bead

Bead Garland

Step 1:
With matching colors, Whipstitch D-F pieces together; with turquoise, Overcast edges.

Athenian Bead

Step 2:
With white, tack pony bead to neck of Pot, leaving needle threaded with white.

Step 3:
Drape bead strand around neck of Pot; with white yarn, catch bead strand on each side of pony bead to hold, then secure yarn end on wrong side.

Step 4:
Glue each end of strand inside one Athenian bead.

Ghostly Greetings

SIZE & MATERIALS

Size: 10" x 13⅛".

Materials: One sheet of 7-count plastic canvas; Worsted-weight or plastic canvas yarn (for amounts see Color Key).

INSTRUCTIONS

Cutting Instructions:
For Ghost, cut one according to graph.

Stitching Instructions:
(Note: C piece is not worked.)
1: Using colors and stitches indicated, work according to graph; fill in uncoded areas using white and Continental Stitch.

2: With matching colors, Overcast edges. Using colors (Separate black into individual strands, if desired.) indicated and Backstitch, embroider detail as indicated on graph.
3: Hang or display as desired.◉

Ghost
(cut 1)
66 x 87 holes

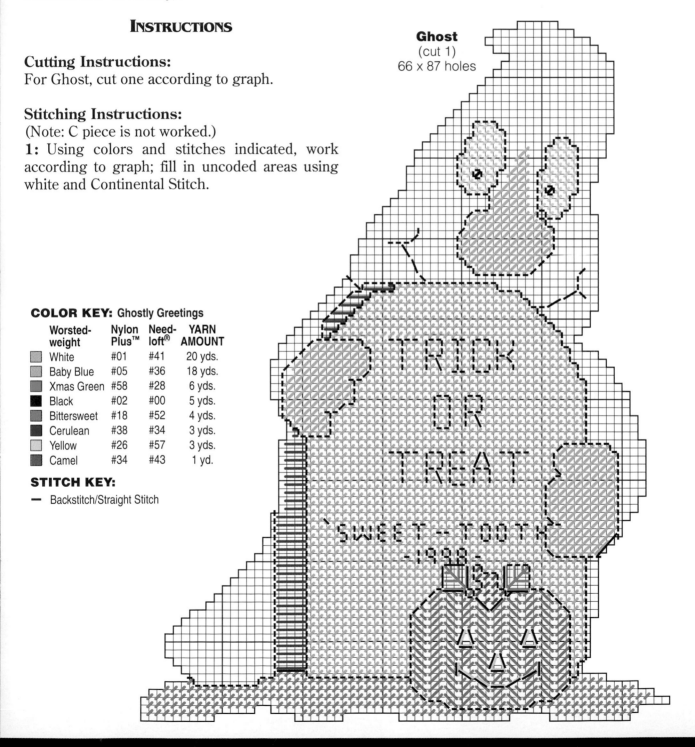

COLOR KEY: Ghostly Greetings

Worsted-weight	Nylon Plus™	Need-loft®	YARN AMOUNT
White	#01	#41	20 yds.
Baby Blue	#05	#36	18 yds.
Xmas Green	#58	#28	6 yds.
Black	#02	#00	5 yds.
Bittersweet	#18	#52	4 yds.
Cerulean	#38	#34	3 yds.
Yellow	#26	#57	3 yds.
Camel	#34	#43	1 yd.

STITCH KEY:
— Backstitch/Straight Stitch

Treat your
furry friends
to mealtime fun.

Pet Food Pals

SIZE & MATERIALS

Sizes: Dog is 4¾" x 3" x 9½" tall; Cat is 5⅜" x 2⅞" x 8⅞" tall. Each fits within a 4⅞" x 10½" x 1½" tall pet food dish.

Materials For One: 1½ sheets of 7-count plastic canvas; Three craft or ice cream sticks; Craft glue or glue gun; Metallic cord (for amount see Dog Color Key on page 59); Worsted-weight or plastic canvas yarn (for amounts see individual Color Keys on pages 58 & 59).

CAT INSTRUCTIONS

Cutting Instructions:
(Note: Graphs on pages 58 & 59.)
A: For front and backing, cut two (one for front and one for backing) according to graph.
B: For base pieces, cut two 19 x 29 holes.
C: For dish brace pieces, cut three 9 x 29 holes (no graph).
D: For mouse body, cut one according to graph.
E: For mouse ears, cut two according to graph.

Stitching Instructions:
(Note: Backing A, B and C pieces are not worked.)
1: Using colors and stitches indicated, work one A for front according to graph; fill in uncoded areas using pumpkin and Continental Stitch. Using colors and stitches indicated, work D and one E piece according to graphs; substituting gray for watermelon, work remaining E piece according to graph. With gray, Overcast edges of D and E pieces, leaving a 6" tail at bottom edge of D as indicated on graph.
2: Using colors (Separate into individual plies, if desired.) and embroidery stitches indicated, embroider detail on front A and D as indicated.
3: Thread D tail on needle; run needle from front to back at ◆ hole, then from back to front at ☆

hole as indicated, allowing D to hang about ¼" from A. Knot opposite end of tail and trim end close to knot. Tack pink E to right side of D as indicated; glue gray E to wrong side of D.
4: Glue craft or ice cream sticks to wrong side of front A as indicated. Holding backing A to wrong side of front A, with matching colors, Whipstitch together as indicated; Overcast remaining side edges of front and backing.
5: With pumpkin, Whipstitch and assemble A-C pieces as indicated and according to Cat Assembly Diagram on page 58.
6: Place inner long edge of dish over brace.

DOG INSTRUCTIONS

Cutting Instructions:
(Note: Graphs on page 59.)
A: For front and backing, cut two (one for front and one for backing) according to graph.
B: For base pieces, cut two 19 x 31 holes.
C: For dish brace pieces, cut three 9 x 31 holes (no graph).

Stitching Instructions:
(Note: Backing A, B and C pieces are not worked.)
1: Using colors and stitches indicated, work one A for front according to graph; fill in uncoded areas using white and Continental Stitch.
2: Using colors (Separate yarn into individual plies, if desired.) and embroidery stitches indicated, embroider detail as indicated on graph.
3: Glue craft or ice cream sticks to wrong side of front A as indicated. Holding backing A to wrong side of front A, with matching colors, Whipstitch together as indicated; Overcast remaining side edges of front and backing.
4: Substituting Dog pieces for Cat pieces, with white, Whipstitch and assemble pieces as indicated and according to Cat Assembly Diagram.
5: Place inner long edge of dish over brace.⊛

Pet Food Pals

Instructions & photo on pages 56 & 57.

A – Cat Front & Backing
(cut 1 each) 35 x 57 holes

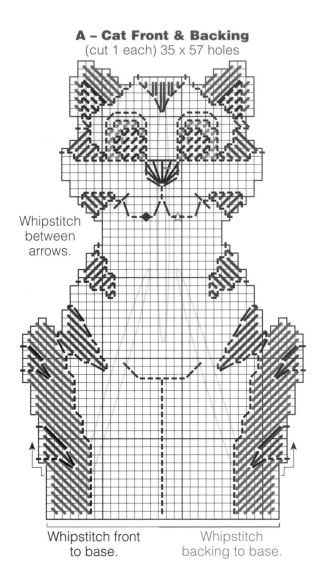

Whipstitch between arrows.

Whipstitch front to base.

Whipstitch backing to base.

B – Cat Base Piece
(cut 2) 19 x 29 holes

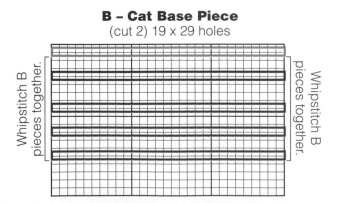

Whipstitch B pieces together.

Whipstitch B pieces together.

COLOR KEY: Cat

	Worsted-weight	Nylon Plus™	Need-loft®	YARN AMOUNT
	Pumpkin	#50	#12	26 yds.
	Black	#02	#00	7 yds.
	Maple	#35	#13	7 yds.
	Gray	#23	#38	2 yds.
	Watermelon	#54	#55	2 yds.
	White	#01	#41	2 yds.

STITCH KEY:

- — Backstitch/Straight Stitch
- ▼ Ear Attachment
- ◊ Craft or Ice Cream Stick Placement
- □ Backing/Base Attachment
- □ Front/Base Attachment
- □ Brace/Base Attachment

Cat Assembly Diagram
(Pieces are shown in different colors for contrast.)

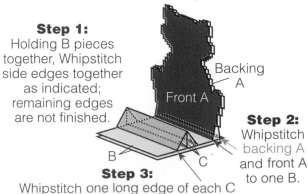

Step 1:
Holding B pieces together, Whipstitch side edges together as indicated; remaining edges are not finished.

Backing A

Front A

B

C

Step 2:
Whipstitch backing A and front A to one B.

Step 3:
Whipstitch one long edge of each C piece to A; Whipstitch C pieces together along top edge.

A – Dog Front & Backing
(cut 1 each) 31 x 61 holes

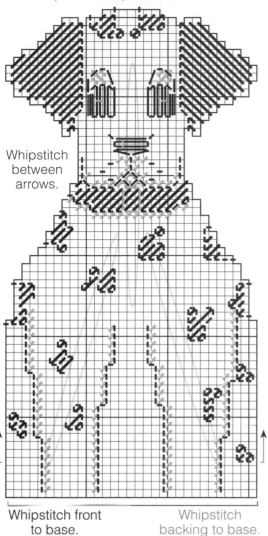

Whipstitch between arrows.

Whipstitch front to base.

Whipstitch backing to base.

COLOR KEY: Dog

	Metallic cord			AMOUNT
	Silver			1 yd.

	Worsted-weight	Nylon Plus™	Need-loft®	YARN AMOUNT
	White	#01	#41	22 yds.
	Black	#02	#00	10 yds.
	Silver	–	#37	4 yds.
	Xmas Red	#19	#02	2 yds.

STITCH KEY:

— Backstitch/Straight Stitch
〇 Craft or Ice Cream Stick Placement
▢ Backing/Base Attachment
▢ Front/Base Attachment
▢ Brace/Base Attachment

D – Mouse Body
(cut 1)
3 x 9 holes

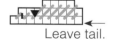

Leave tail.

E – Mouse Ear
(cut 2)
3 x 3 holes

Tack to D.

B – Dog Base Piece
(cut 2) 19 x 31 holes

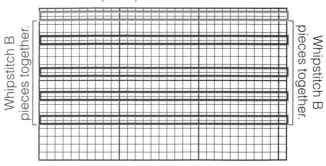

Whipstitch B pieces together.

Whipstitch B pieces together.

Witches' Fun Jar

SIZE & MATERIALS

Size: Assembly is 12½" tall and fits over a 6⅝" tall (60 oz.) jar with a 4" wide lid.

Materials: One sheet of orange, ½ sheet each of clear and black and scraps of white and green 7-count plastic canvas; Two 6" plastic canvas radial circles; 10" x 22" piece of black fabric; Two 9mm blue/black animal eyes (cut off shanks and file nubs smooth); Two 7mm wiggle eyes; One green and two white ¾" pom-poms; Jar (see Size above); Sewing machine or needle and black thread; Craft glue or glue gun; Six-strand embroidery floss (for amount see Color Key on page 62); Raffia straw (for amounts see Color Key); Worsted-weight or plastic canvas yarn (for amounts see Color Key).

INSTRUCTIONS

Cutting Instructions:
(Note: Graphs on pages 62 & 63.)
A: For pumpkin strips, cut twelve from orange according to graph.
B: For pumpkin eye backs, cut two from white according to graph.
C: For pumpkin eye fronts, cut two from black according to graph.
D: For pumpkin nose back, cut one from white according to graph.
E: For pumpkin nose front, cut one from black according to graph.
F: For pumpkin mouth back, cut one from white according to graph.
G: For pumpkin mouth front, cut one from black according to graph.
H: For pumpkin bottom, cut away outer two rows of holes from one circle (no graph).
I: For lid top, cut one from remaining circle according to graph.
J: For lid side, cut one from clear 4 x 90 holes.
K: For witch front and back, cut one from clear for front and one from black for back according to graphs.
L: For witch arms #1 and #2, cut one each from clear according to graphs.
M: For frog back legs, cut one from green according to graph.
N: For frog front legs, cut two from green according to graph.

Stitching Instructions:
(Note: A-H, back K, M and N pieces are not worked.)
1: Using colors and stitches indicated, work I, J (overlap holes as indicated on graph and work through both thicknesses at overlap area to join ends), front K and L pieces according to graphs. With matching colors, Overcast bottom edge of front K as indicated and edges of L pieces.
2: Using three strands floss and embroidery stitches indicated, embroider facial features on front K as indicated.
3: For witch, holding back K to wrong side of front K, with matching colors, Whipstitch matching edges together.
4: For each pumpkin eye, matching outside edges, glue one C to one B; repeat with D-G pieces for nose and mouth.
5: For pumpkin, with orange raffia, Whipstitch and assemble A and H pieces and jar according to Pumpkin Assembly Diagram on page 62; glue eyes, nose and mouth to strips as shown in photo.
6: For cape, sew fabric according to Cape Assembly Diagram on page 63.
7: Whipstitch and assemble witch, cape, I, J and L pieces according to Witch Lid Assembly Diagram on page 63.
8: For frog, assemble green pom-pom, wiggle eyes, black yarn and M and N pieces according to Frog Assembly Diagram on page 62. Glue one animal eye to each white pom-pom; glue pom-poms and frog to lid top as shown. Lid fits snugly over jar lid.

◼️ Witches' Fun Jar

Instructions & photo on pages 60 & 61.

COLOR KEY: Witches' Fun Jar

Embroidery floss			AMOUNT
◼️ Black			2 yds.
Raffia straw			**AMOUNT**
◻️ Lt. Green			14 yds.
◻️ Black			8 yds.
◼️ Orange			6 yds.
◼️ Purple			4 yds.
◻️ White			1 yd.

	Worsted-weight	Nylon Plus™	Need-loft®	YARN AMOUNT
◻️	Coral	#14	#66	6 yds.
◻️	Black	#02	#00	1/4 yd.

STITCH KEY:
— Backstitch/Straight Stitch
• French Knot

A – Pumpkin Strip
(cut 12 from orange)
5 x 43 holes

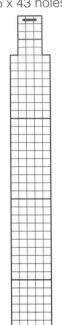

Whipstitch to H.

B – Pumpkin Eye Back
(cut 2 from white)
7 x 9 holes

C – Pumpkin Eye Front
(cut 2 from black)
7 x 9 holes

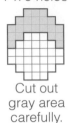

Cut out gray area carefully.

D – Pumpkin Nose Back
(cut 1 from white)
7 x 10 holes

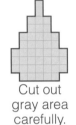

E – Pumpkin Nose Front
(cut 1 from black)
7 x 10 holes

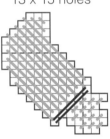

Cut out gray area carefully.

L – Witch Arm #1
(cut 1 from clear)
13 x 15 holes

L – Witch Arm #2
(cut 1 from clear)
13 x 15 holes

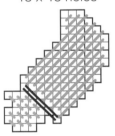

G – Pumpkin Mouth Front
(cut 1 from black)
8 x 23 holes

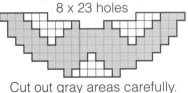

Cut out gray areas carefully.

F – Pumpkin Mouth Back
(cut 1 from white)
8 x 23 holes

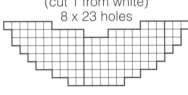

N – Frog Front Leg
(cut 2 from green)
2 x 2 holes

Pumpkin Assembly Diagram
(Some pieces are shown in different colors for contrast.)

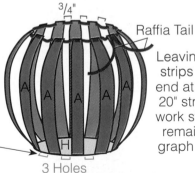

3/4"

Raffia Tail

3 Holes

Step 1:
Leaving three holes between strips, Whipstitch A pieces to H, Overcasting H between strips as you work.

Step 2:
Leaving about 3/4" between strips and a 6" tail at each end at front of one A, with a 20" strand of orange raffia, work stitches at top of each remaining A according to graph to loosely join strips.

Step 3:
Place jar inside assembly; pulling ends carefully to even, tighten strips around neck of jar.

Step 4:
Tie tails into a bow and trim ends; pull raffia gently to widen bow loops and tails.

M – Frog Back Legs
(cut 1 from green)
3 x 9 holes

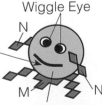

Frog Assembly Diagram

Step 1:
Glue a 3/4" length of black yarn to green pom-pom for mouth.

Step 2:
Glue wiggle eyes, M and N pieces to pom-pom.

Wiggle Eye

N

M   N

Green Pom-pom

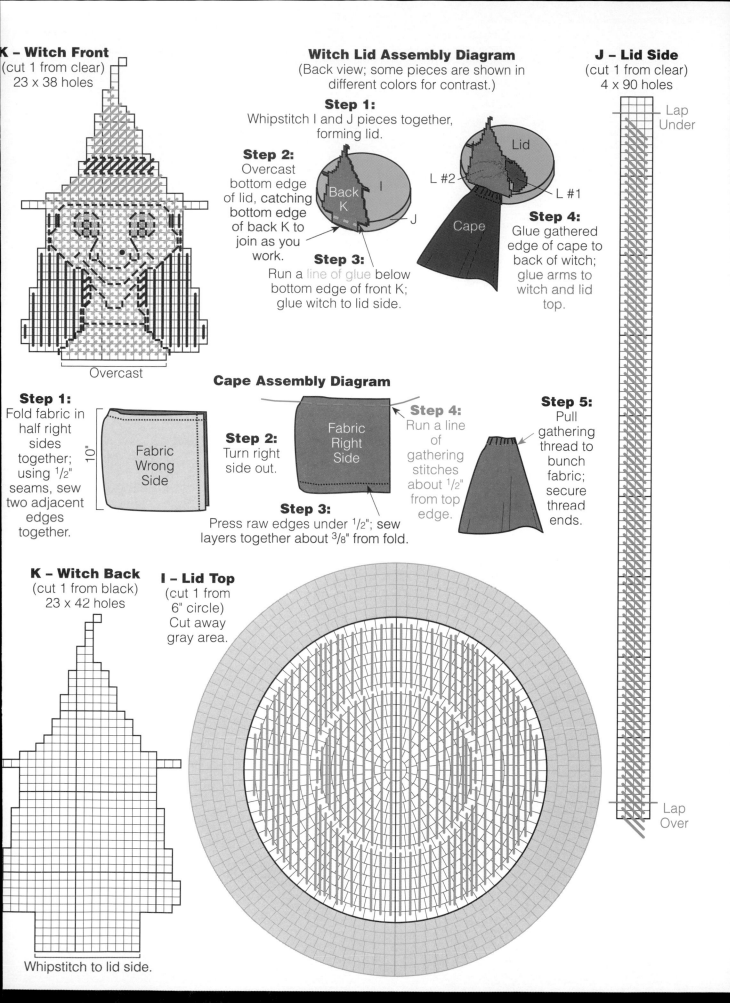

K – Witch Front
(cut 1 from clear)
23 x 38 holes

Overcast

Witch Lid Assembly Diagram
(Back view; some pieces are shown in different colors for contrast.)

Step 1:
Whipstitch I and J pieces together, forming lid.

Step 2:
Overcast bottom edge of lid, catching bottom edge of back K to join as you work.

Step 3:
Run a line of glue below bottom edge of front K; glue witch to lid side.

Back K

I

J

Lid

L #2

L #1

Cape

Step 4:
Glue gathered edge of cape to back of witch; glue arms to witch and lid top.

J – Lid Side
(cut 1 from clear)
4 x 90 holes

Lap Under

Lap Over

Cape Assembly Diagram

Step 1:
Fold fabric in half right sides together; using 1/2" seams, sew two adjacent edges together.

10"

Fabric Wrong Side

Step 2:
Turn right side out.

Fabric Right Side

Step 3:
Press raw edges under 1/2"; sew layers together about 3/8" from fold.

Step 4:
Run a line of gathering stitches about 1/2" from top edge.

Step 5:
Pull gathering thread to bunch fabric; secure thread ends.

K – Witch Back
(cut 1 from black)
23 x 42 holes

Whipstitch to lid side.

I – Lid Top
(cut 1 from 6" circle)
Cut away gray area.

CHAPTER 4

Michele Wilcox

**D**esigner Michele Wilcox has been at the forefront of new plastic canvas design trends since the late 1980s. Reflecting on the many steps that make up the design process, Michele says that she is very possessive of her projects from start to finish. Though many professional designers hire stitchers to complete items that are past the conceptual phase, Michele prefers to work each and every stitch herself. She likes quick and easy designs and uses bright colors sparingly. Many of her ideas come from greeting cards, and her unique style keeps Michele a trendsetter in the world of needlework.

Having recently been blessed with her first grandbaby, Michele spent several weeks knitting booties. And, she assures us, a plastic canvas nursery set is definitely in the works.

Michele and her husband, Dick, are residents of Massachusetts. Their home is in an old gate house built in 1896. She and Dick often walk their 30 acres, enjoying wildlife, such as deer and bluebirds. Michele's hobbies include reading, collecting antique novels and watching old movies.

Rainy Day Ducks

SIZE & MATERIALS

Sizes: Doorstop is 2⅝" x 4⅛" x 7⅞" tall; Music Box Duck is 3¾" across x about 6" tall, not including musical movement; Tissue Cover snugly covers a boutique-style tissue box; Doorknob Hanger is 6½" x 9½".

Materials: Seven sheets of 7-count plastic canvas; Brick to fit above dimensions or zip-close bag filled with sand or other weighting material; 1" x 2" x 2" music box with a 3¼"-across round turntable; ⅓ yd. white 2" lace; ⅔ yd. white ½" lace trim; Spanish moss; 6" length of ¼" wooden dowel; Polyester fiberfill; Craft glue or glue gun; #3 pearl cotton or six-strand embroidery floss (for amounts see Color Key on page 69); Worsted-weight or plastic canvas yarn (for amounts see Color Key).

INSTRUCTIONS

Cutting Instructions:

(Note: Graphs on pages 68-70.)

A: For Doorstop front, cut one 26 x 51 holes.

B: For Doorstop back, cut one 26 x 51 holes (no graph).

C: For Doorstop sides, cut two 16 x 51 holes (no graph).

D: For Doorstop top and bottom, cut two (one for top and one for bottom) 16 x 26 holes (no graph).

E: For Music Box tub side, cut one 17 x 69 holes.

F: For Music Box tub bottom, cut one according to graph.

G: For Music Box duck front and back, cut two (one for front and one for back) according to graph.

H: For Music Box duck wings, cut two according to graph.

I: For Music Box duck beak top and bottom, cut two (one for top and one for bottom) according to graph.

J: For Music Box umbrella top, cut one according to graph.

■ Rainy Day Ducks

Continued from page 67.

K: For Tissue Cover sides, cut four 30 x 36 holes.
L: For Tissue Cover top, cut one according to graph.
M: For Tissue Cover ducks #1 and #2, cut one each according to graphs.
N: For Tissue Cover umbrella, cut one according to graph.
O: For Doorknob Hanger, cut one according to graph.

Stitching Instructions:

1: Using colors and stitches indicated, work A-G, H (one on opposite side of canvas) and I-O pieces according to graphs and stitch pattern guide; fill in uncoded areas of A using baby blue and Continental Stitch. With straw, Overcast cutout edges of L; with cinnamon for top and handle of Tissue Cover umbrella and with matching colors, Overcast edges of H-J and M-O pieces.
2: Using yarn and pearl cotton or six strands floss in colors and embroidery stitches indicated, embroider detail on A, one G for front, M and O

pieces as indicated on graphs.
3: For Doorstop, with teal blue yarn, Whipstitch A-D pieces wrong sides together, inserting weight before closing.
(Note: Cut ½"-wide lace trim in half.)
4: Whipstitch and assemble E-I pieces, fiberfill and Spanish moss as indicated and according to Tub & Duck Assembly Diagram. For umbrella, slide one end of dowel through cutout on J and glue to secure. Fold down umbrella sections and glue overlapping corners together (see photo); glue opposite end of dowel to one wing as shown in photo. Glue trim around top and bottom edges of tub as shown.
5: Assemble musical movement and turntable according to manufacturer's instructions; glue tub to turntable. Glue 2" wide lace around underside of turntable as shown for ruffle.
6: For Tissue Cover, with straw, Whipstitch K and L pieces together; Overcast unfinished bottom edges. Glue M and N pieces to one Cover side as shown.◉

O – Doorknob Hanger
(cut 1) 42 x 62 holes

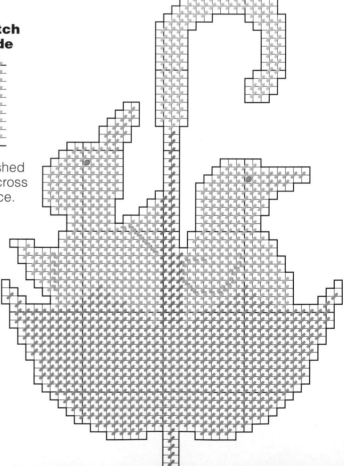

A – Doorstop Front
(cut 1) 26 x 51 holes

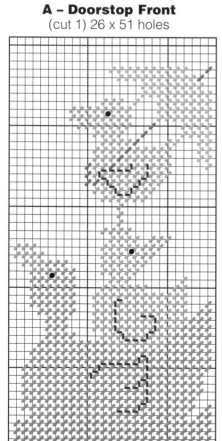

Doorstop Stitch Pattern Guide

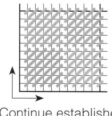

Continue established pattern up and across each entire piece.

F – Music Box Tub Bottom
(cut 1) 22 x 22 holes

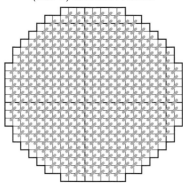

H – Music Box Duck Wing
(cut 2)
8 x 12 holes

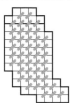

G – Music Box Duck Front & Back
(cut 1 each) 21 x 30 holes

Whipstitch between arrows.

I – Music Box Duck Beak Top & Bottom
(cut 1 each)
4 x 5 holes

Glue

J – Music Box Umbrella Top
(cut 1) 25 x 25 holes

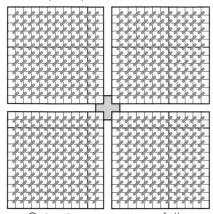

Cut out gray area carefully.

COLOR KEY: Rainy Day Ducks

#3 pearl cotton or floss			AMOUNT
■ Orange			2 yds.
■ Teal			1¹/₂ yds.

Worsted-weight	Nylon Plus™	Need-loft®	YARN AMOUNT
Straw	#41	#19	3¹/₂ oz.
Watermelon	#54	#55	2¹/₂ oz.
Teal Blue	#08	#50	55 yds.
Baby Blue	#05	#36	10 yds.
Pumpkin	#50	#12	10 yds.
Cinnamon	#44	#14	6 yds.
White	#01	#41	6 yds.

STITCH KEY:
— Backstitch/Straight Stitch
• French Knot

Tub & Duck Assembly Diagram

Step 1:
With watermelon, whipstitch short ends of E wrong sides together; whipstitch E and F pieces wrong sides together, and Overcast unfinished edges.

Step 2:
With straw, Whipstitch G pieces wrong sides together; Overcast unfinished bottom edges.

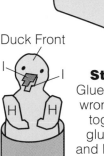

Step 5:
Stuff duck lightly with fiberfill; glue Spanish moss (not shown) and duck inside tub.

Step 4:
Glue I pieces wrong sides together; glue beak and H pieces to duck front.

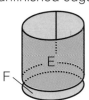

E – Music Box Tub Side (cut 1) 17 x 69 holes

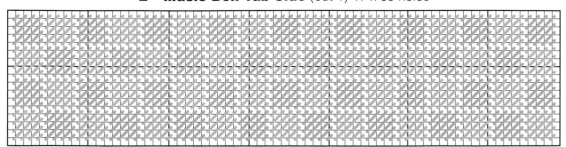

Rainy Day Ducks

Instructions & photo on pages 66 & 67.

K – Tissue Cover Side
(cut 4) 30 x 36 holes

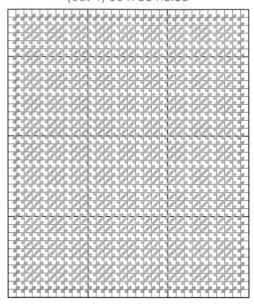

L – Tissue Cover Top
(cut 1) 30 x 30 holes

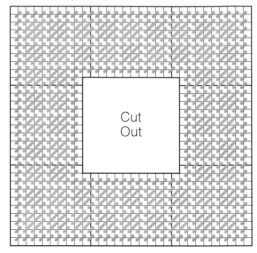

Cut
Out

N – Tissue Cover Umbrella
(cut 1) 31 x 32 holes

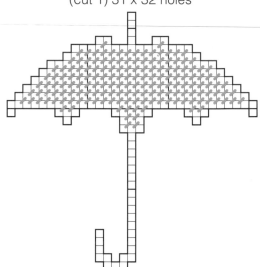

COLOR KEY: Rainy Day Ducks

#3 pearl cotton or floss			AMOUNT
■ Orange			2 yds.
■ Teal			1¹/₂ yds.

Worsted-weight	Nylon Plus™	Need-loft®	YARN AMOUNT
Straw	#41	#19	3¹/₂ oz.
Watermelon	#54	#55	2¹/₂ oz.
Teal Blue	#08	#50	55 yds.
Baby Blue	#05	#36	10 yds.
Pumpkin	#50	#12	10 yds.
Cinnamon	#44	#14	6 yds.
White	#01	#41	6 yds.

STITCH KEY:

— Backstitch/Straight Stitch

● French Knot

M – Tissue Cover Duck #1
(cut 1) 18 x 19 holes

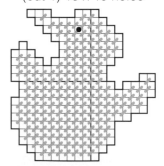

M – Tissue Cover Duck #2
(cut 1) 18 x 19 holes

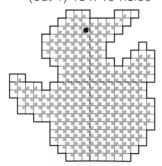

Cuddly Honey Bear

SIZE & MATERIALS

Size: Doorstop is 2¾" x 7⅞" x 8⅛" tall, including motif.

Materials: Two sheets of 7-count plastic canvas; Six small pink silk rosebuds with leaves; Brick to fit above dimensions or a zip-close bag filled with sand or other weighting material; Craft glue or glue gun; #3 pearl cotton or six-strand embroidery floss (for amount see Color Key on page 72); Worsted-weight or plastic canvas yarn (for amounts see Color Key).

INSTRUCTIONS

Cutting Instructions:
(Note: Graphs on page 72.)
A: For sides, cut two 26 x 51 holes.
B: For ends, cut two 16 x 26 holes.
C: For top and bottom, cut two (one for top and one for bottom) 16 x 51 holes.
D: For bear, cut one according to graph.
E: For bear arms, cut two according to graph.
F: For bow, cut one according to graph.

Stitching Instructions:
1: Using colors and stitches indicated, work A-D and F pieces according to graphs; fill in uncoded areas of D, and work E pieces on opposite sides of canvas using camel and Continental Stitch. With camel for feet and ears and with matching colors, Overcast edges of D-F pieces.
2: Using pearl cotton or six strands floss and embroidery stitches indicated, embroider facial detail on D as indicated on graph.
3: With pink, Whipstitch A-C pieces wrong sides together, inserting weight before closing.
4: Matching bottom edges, glue bear to one side; glue rosebuds, arms and bow to bear as shown in photo.✲

Cuddly Honey Bear

Instructions & photo on page 71.

D – Bear
(cut 1) 44 x 50 holes

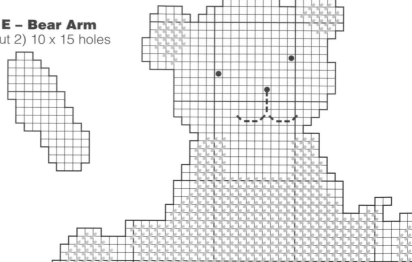

E – Bear Arm
(cut 2) 10 x 15 holes

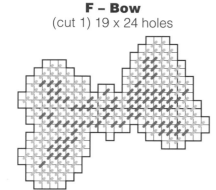

F – Bow
(cut 1) 19 x 24 holes

B – End
(cut 2) 16 x 26 holes

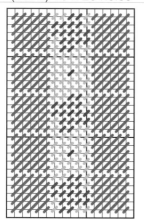

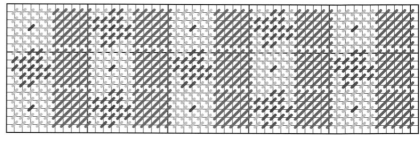

C – Top & Bottom (cut 1 each) 16 x 51 holes

COLOR KEY: Cuddly Honey Bear

#3 pearl cotton or floss			AMOUNT
■ Black			1 yd.

Worsted-weight	Nylon Plus™	Need-loft®	YARN AMOUNT
Cerulean	#38	#34	35 yds.
Lavender	#12	#05	30 yds.
Denim	#06	#33	25 yds.
Pink	#11	#07	25 yds.
Camel	#34	#43	18 yds.
Tangerine	#15	#11	5 yds.
Coral	#14	#66	4 yds.

STITCH KEY:

– Backstitch/Straight Stitch
● French Knot

A – Side (cut 2) 26 x 51 holes

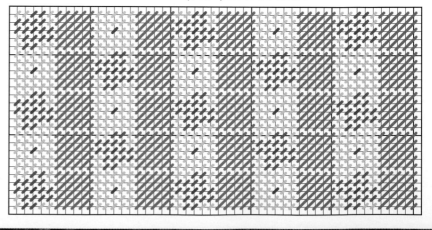

Christmas Charms

Instructions on next page

Capture the joy of Christmas with these seasonal decorations.

■ Christmas Charms

Photo on page 73.

SIZE & MATERIALS

Sizes: Gingerbread Boy is 9¾" x 13¼"; each Coaster is 4½" x 5".

Materials: Four sheets of 7-count plastic canvas; Yellow ½" button; 10 antique gold 10mm fluted beads; Six silver 6mm round beads; Size 18 tapestry needle; 1½ yds. green ¼" satin ribbon; #3 pearl cotton or six-strand embroidery floss (for amounts see Color Key); Worsted-weight or plastic canvas yarn (for amounts see Color Key).

INSTRUCTIONS

Cutting Instructions:

A: For Gingerbread Boy front and backing, cut two (one for front and one for backing) according to graph.

B: For mittens, cut one each according to graphs.

C: For Coasters, cut four according to graph.

Stitching Instructions:

(Note: One A is not worked for backing.)

1: Using colors and stitches indicated, work one A for front, B and C pieces according to graphs. Fill in uncoded areas of A using camel and Continental Stitch; fill in uncoded areas of C pieces using white and Continental Stitch. With matching colors, Overcast edges of B and C pieces.

2: Using pearl cotton or six strands floss in colors and embroidery stitches indicated, embroider detail on front A and C pieces as indicated on graphs.

(Note: Cut one 18" length of red pearl cotton or six-strand floss.)

3: Tie a knot in one end of red strand, and with size 18 needle, thread strand from back to front through one ▲ hole on A as indicated; thread strand through beads and through ★ holes on each B piece as indicated and according to Bead & Mitten Assembly Illustration, then thread strand end from front to back through adjacent ▲ hole on A as indicated. Knot end on wrong side to secure.

4: Glue, or with white pearl cotton or floss, sew button to front A as indicated. Holding backing A to wrong side of front A, with camel, Whipstitch together.

(Note: Cut ribbon into one 1-yd. and one ½-yd. length.)

5: For hanger, thread short ribbon through ✦ holes on A as indicated and tie ends into a bow. Thread long ribbon through cutouts on Coasters and tie into a bow to secure.❀

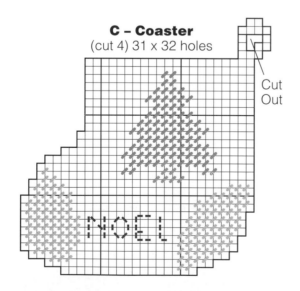

C – Coaster
(cut 4) 31 x 32 holes

Cut Out

COLOR KEY: Christmas Charms

#3 pearl cotton or floss			AMOUNT
■ Red			3 yds.
■ Black			¼ yd.
■ White			¼ yd.

Worsted-weight	Nylon Plus™	Need-loft®	YARN AMOUNT
Camel	#34	#43	48 yds.
White	#01	#41	45 yds.
Red	#20	#01	30 yds.
Xmas Green	#58	#28	19 yds.
Black	#02	#00	1 yd.

STITCH KEY:

— Backstitch/Straight Stitch

● French Knot

♥ Button Attachment

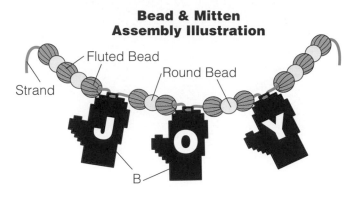

Bead & Mitten
Assembly Illustration

Strand — Fluted Bead — Round Bead

J O Y

B

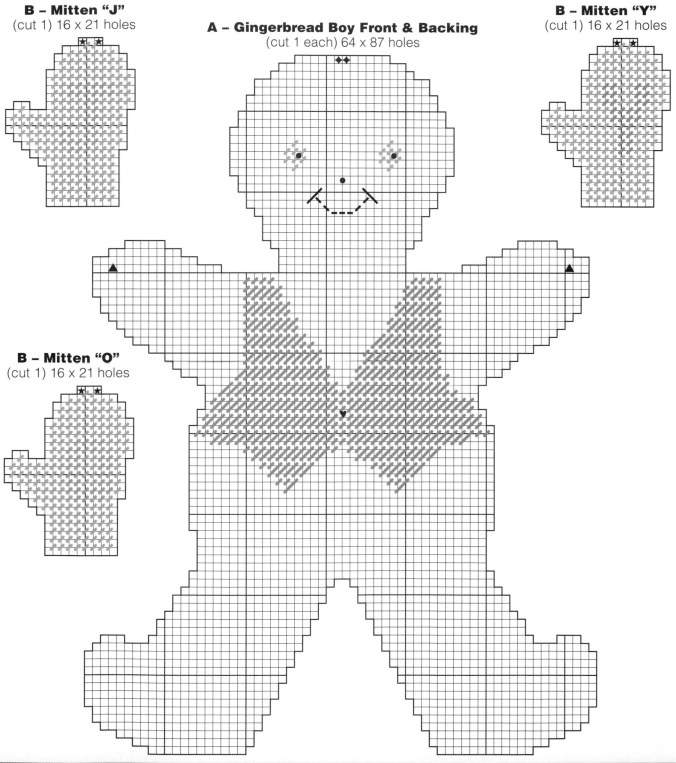

B – Mitten "J"
(cut 1) 16 x 21 holes

A – Gingerbread Boy Front & Backing
(cut 1 each) 64 x 87 holes

B – Mitten "Y"
(cut 1) 16 x 21 holes

B – Mitten "O"
(cut 1) 16 x 21 holes

Nesting Bluebirds

SIZE & MATERIALS

Sizes: Doily is 10⅜" x 18⅝"; Tissue Cover snugly covers a boutique-style tissue box.

Materials: One 13½" x 22½" and 1½ standard-size sheets of 7-count plastic canvas; #3 pearl cotton or six-strand embroidery floss (for amount see Color Key); Worsted-weight or plastic canvas yarn (for amounts see Color Key).

INSTRUCTIONS

Cutting Instructions:

A: For Doily, cut one from large canvas sheet according to graph on page 78.

B: For Tissue Cover sides, cut four 30 x 36 holes.

C: For Tissue Cover top, cut one according to graph.

Stitching Instructions:

1: Using colors indicated and Continental Stitch, work pieces according to graphs. Fill in uncoded areas of A using eggshell and Continental Stitch; fill in uncoded areas of B and C pieces using baby yellow and Continental Stitch. With matching colors, Overcast edges of A; with baby yellow, Over-cast cutout edges of C.

2: Using pearl cotton or six strands floss and French Knot, embroider eyes on A and B pieces as indicated on graphs.

3: With baby yellow, Whipstitch B and C pieces together, forming Cover; Overcast unfinished bottom edges.◉

B – Tissue Cover Side
(cut 4) 30 x 36 holes

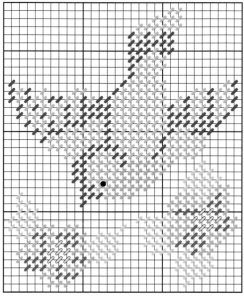

C – Tissue Cover Top
(cut 1) 30 x 30 holes

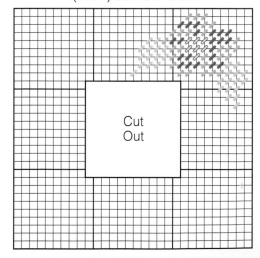

COLOR KEY: Nesting Bluebirds

#3 pearl cotton or floss			AMOUNT
■ Black			2 yds.

Worsted-weight	Nylon Plus™	Need-loft®	YARN AMOUNT
☐ Baby Yellow	#42	#21	55 yds.
▨ Lilac	#22	#45	30 yds.
▨ Sail Blue	#04	#35	30 yds.
▨ Mermaid Green	#37	#53	28 yds.
▨ Royal	#09	#32	22 yds.
☐ Eggshell	#24	#39	20 yds.
▨ Lavender	#12	#05	10 yds.
▨ Pink	#11	#07	10 yds.
▨ Pumpkin	#50	#12	9 yds.
▨ Straw	#41	#19	8 yds.
▨ Forest	#32	#29	6 yds.

STITCH KEY:

● French Knot

Nesting Bluebirds

Instructions and photo on pages 76 & 77.

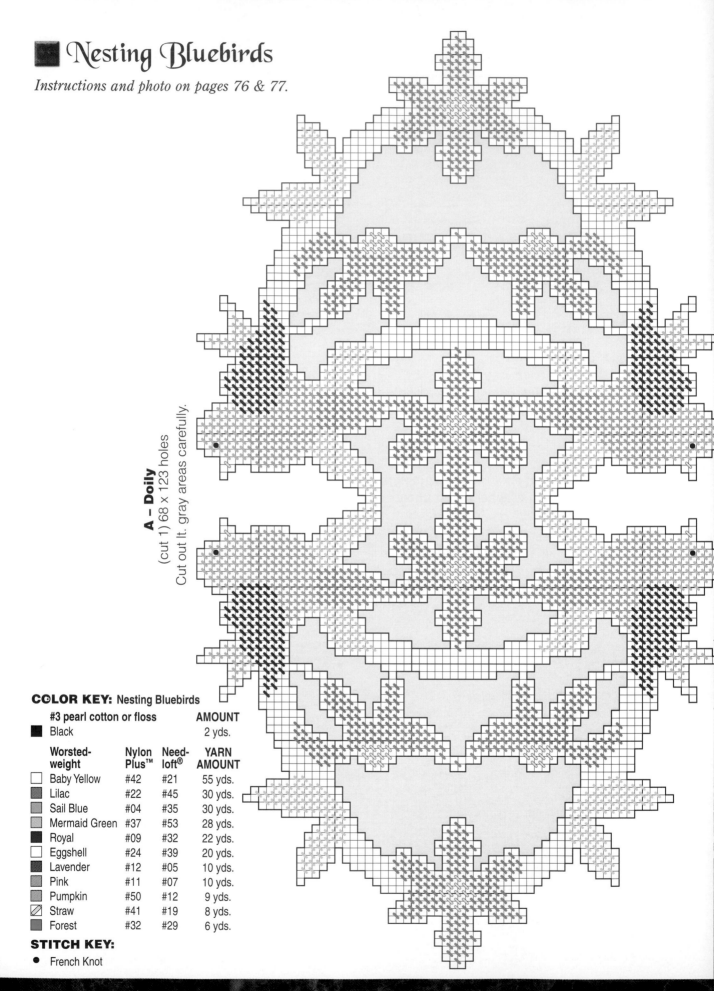

A – Doily
(cut 1) 68 x 123 holes
Cut out lt. gray areas carefully.

COLOR KEY: Nesting Bluebirds

#3 pearl cotton or floss			AMOUNT
■ Black			2 yds.

Worsted-weight	Nylon Plus™	Need-loft®	YARN AMOUNT
Baby Yellow	#42	#21	55 yds.
Lilac	#22	#45	30 yds.
Sail Blue	#04	#35	30 yds.
Mermaid Green	#37	#53	28 yds.
Royal	#09	#32	22 yds.
Eggshell	#24	#39	20 yds.
Lavender	#12	#05	10 yds.
Pink	#11	#07	10 yds.
Pumpkin	#50	#12	9 yds.
Straw	#41	#19	8 yds.
Forest	#32	#29	6 yds.

STITCH KEY:

● French Knot

SIZE & MATERIALS

Size: Snugly covers a boutique-style tissue box.

Materials: 2½ sheets of 7-count plastic canvas; Craft glue or glue gun; #3 pearl cotton or six-strand embroidery floss (for amounts see Color Key); Worsted-weight or plastic canvas yarn (for amounts see Color Key).

INSTRUCTIONS

Cutting Instructions:
(Note: Graphs continued on page 81.)
A: For sides, cut four 30 x 36 holes.
B: For top, cut one according to graph.
C: For teapot, cut one according to graph.
D: For green teacup, cut one according to graph.
E: For green saucer, cut one according to graph.
F: For turquoise teacup, cut one according to graph.
G: For turquoise saucer, cut one according to graph.

Stitching Instructions:
1: Using colors and stitches indicated, work pieces according to graphs. With matching colors, Overcast edges of C-G pieces and cutout edges of B.

2: Using pearl cotton or six strands floss in colors and embroidery stitches indicated, embroider detail on C, D and F pieces as indicated on graphs.
3: With straw, Whipstitch A and B pieces together, forming Cover; with white, Overcast unfinished bottom edges. Glue teapot, teacups and saucers to one Cover side as shown in photo.⊛

D – Green Teacup
(cut 1) 10 x 16 holes

E – Green Saucer
(cut 1) 4 x 20 holes

C – Teapot
(cut 1) 31 x 41 holes

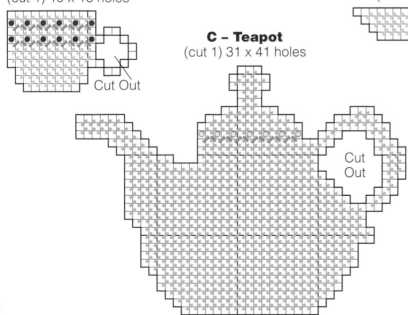

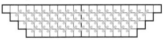

COLOR KEY: Tea Time

#3 pearl cotton or floss			AMOUNT
▨ Green			2 yds.
■ Pink			2 yds.
☐ Yellow			2 yds.
■ Blue			1 yd.

Worsted-weight	Nylon Plus™	Need-loft®	YARN AMOUNT
☐ Straw	#41	#19	50 yds.
☐ White	#01	#41	50 yds.
☐ Watermelon	#54	#55	12 yds.
☐ Baby Green	#28	#26	6 yds.
☐ Turquoise	#03	#54	6 yds.

STITCH KEY:
— Backstitch/Straight Stitch
● French Knot

April Showers

SIZE & MATERIALS

Size: 6⅛" x 13⅛".

Materials: One sheet of 7-count plastic canvas; Craft glue or glue gun; Worsted-weight or plastic canvas yarn (for amounts see Color Key).

INSTRUCTIONS

Cutting Instructions:
A: For frog, cut one according to graph.
B: For umbrella, cut one according to graph.

Stitching Instructions:
1: Using colors indicated and Continental Stitch, work pieces according to graphs. With holly for frog body, black for umbrella top and handle and with matching colors, Overcast edges of pieces.
2: Using black and embroidery stitches indicated, embroider facial detail on A as indicated on graph.
3: Glue umbrella handle to raised arm of frog as shown in photo.⊛

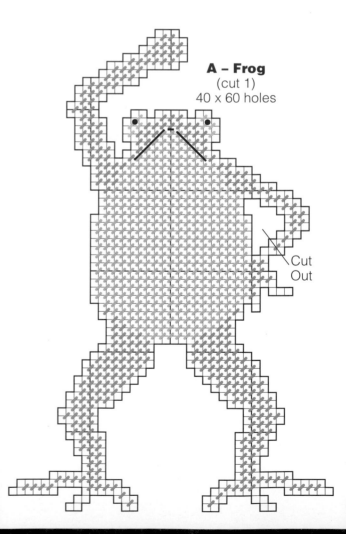

A – Frog
(cut 1)
40 x 60 holes

Cut Out

B – Umbrella
(cut 1) 27 x 34 holes

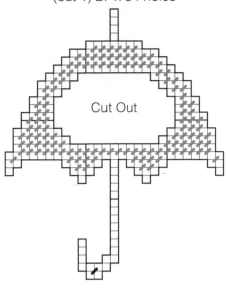

Cut Out

COLOR KEY: April Showers

	Worsted-weight	Nylon Plus™	Need-loft®	YARN AMOUNT
	Holly	#31	#27	15 yds.
	Baby Yellow	#42	#21	10 yds.
	Tangerine	#15	#11	6 yds.
	Black	#02	#00	2 yds.
	White	#01	#41	1 yd.

STITCH KEY:
— Backstitch/Straight Stitch
• French Knot

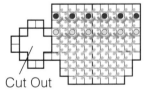

Tea Time

Instructions & photo on page 79.

COLOR KEY: Tea Time

	#3 pearl cotton or floss			AMOUNT
	Green			2 yds.
	Pink			2 yds.
	Yellow			2 yds.
	Blue			1 yd.

	Worsted-weight	Nylon Plus™	Need-loft®	YARN AMOUNT
	Straw	#41	#19	50 yds.
	White	#01	#41	50 yds.
	Watermelon	#54	#55	12 yds.
	Baby Green	#28	#26	6 yds.
	Turquoise	#03	#54	6 yds.

STITCH KEY:
— Backstitch/Straight Stitch
• French Knot

F – Turquoise Teacup
(cut 1) 10 x 16 holes

Cut Out

G – Turquoise Saucer
(cut 1) 4 x 20 holes

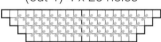

A – Side
(cut 4) 30 x 36 holes

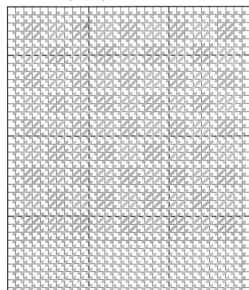

B – Top
(cut 1) 30 x 30 holes

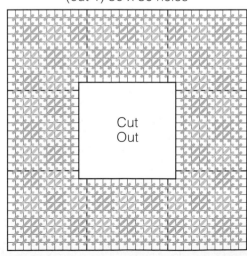

Cut Out

CHAPTER 5

Debbie
Tabor

Designer Debbie Tabor has been designing professionally for nearly 10 years. She credits her mother for encouraging her interest in needlework, and Debbie has been crafting since the tender age of eight.

Debbie and her husband, Brian, are the parents of 13-year-old Mandy and eight-year-old Christopher. Brian owns a business, and Debbie spends much of her time helping out by answering phones, bookkeeping and even hanging rain gutters. Quite the busy mom, Debbie is also very involved with her children's education. As a volunteer at their school, she goes on field trips, helps with parties, and once helped her son dissect a cow's eye in science class.

Her popular designs reflect the loves of Debbie's life. She is a collector of anything that makes her smile, and she especially enjoys collecting pigs. When she is not designing, Debbie spends her free time gardening. Most of her gardening time, Debbie notes, is spent keeping the family dog away from her work.

The Tabors and their English Springer Spaniel, Lady, make their home in Colorado.

Enjoy the handy convenience of this heavenly organizer.

Baby's Angel Organizer

SIZE & MATERIALS

Size: 3¾" x 9½" x 11¼".

Materials: Two sheets of 7-count plastic canvas; 19 green ⅞" silk leaves; Three cream, five baby pink and five baby blue ⅞" satin ribbon roses; Craft glue or glue gun; Six-strand embroidery floss (for amounts see Color Key); Worsted-weight or plastic canvas yarn (for amounts see Color Key).

INSTRUCTIONS

Cutting Instructions:
(Note: Graphs continued on pages 86 & 87.)
A: For front, cut one according to graph.
B: For back, cut one according to graph.
C: For outer sides, cut two according to graph.
D: For inner sides, cut two 21 x 29 holes.

E: For bottom, cut one according to graph.

Stitching Instructions:
(Note: E piece is not worked.)
1: Using colors and stitches indicated and leaving uncoded and attachment areas unworked, work B-D (one C on opposite side of canvas) pieces according to graphs; using white and Continental Stitch, work A. Fill in uncoded hair area on B using straw and Bullion Knots; with straw, Overcast edges of hair area.
2: Using six strands floss in colors and embroidery stitches indicated, embroider detail on A and B pieces as indicated on graphs; with white, Whipstitch A-E pieces together as indicated and according to Organizer Assembly Diagram; Overcast unfinished edges.
3: Glue leaves and roses across Angel's head as shown in photo.⊛

COLOR KEY: Baby's Angel

Embroidery floss			AMOUNT
⬛ Black			7 yds.
⬛ Gray			7 yds.
⬛ Yellow			7 yds.
⬛ Royal Blue			1 yd.
⬛ Sky Blue			½ yd.
▨ White			½ yd.

Iridescent yarn			AMOUNT
⬛ White			14 yds.

Worsted-weight	Nylon Plus™	Need-loft®	YARN AMOUNT
⬜ White	#01	#41	70 yds.
⬛ Straw	#41	#19	12 yds.
⬜ Peach	#46	#47	9 yds.
⬛ Pink	#11	#07	2 yds.
⬛ Black	#02	#00	1 yd.
⬜ Bt. Blue	–	#60	1 yd.

Organizer Assembly Diagram

Step 3:
Bending C pieces to fit, Whipstitch C pieces and assembly together.

Step 2:
Whipstitch A, B, D and E pieces together.

Step 1:
Whipstitch bottom edges of D pieces to E.

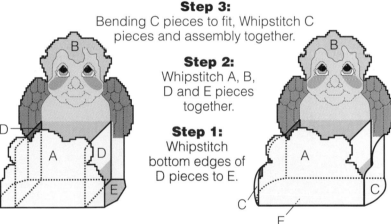

E – Bottom
(cut 1) 21 x 63 holes

Whipstitch to one C.

Whipstitch to one C.

Baby's Angel Organizer

Instructions & photo on pages 84 & 85.

A – Front
(cut 1) 40 x 54 holes

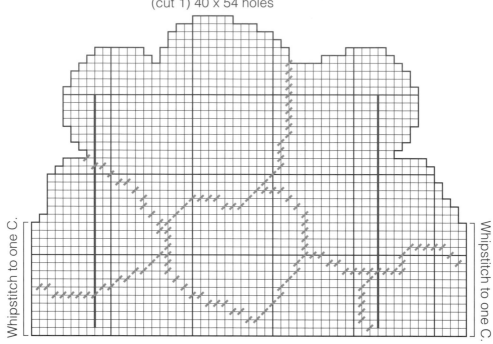

Whipstitch to one C.

Whipstitch to one C.

Bullion Knot Stitch Diagram

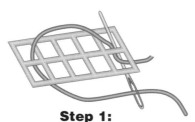

Step 1:
Come up through one hole on canvas and back down at a second hole several holes away, depending on the desired size and direction of the knot, leaving a loop; come up through first hole again with needle tip only.

Step 3:
Draw the needle through the twists and gently pull the yarn through.

Step 2:
Wrap the loop around the needle tip until the twists equal the distance between the two holes.

Step 4:
Go down again at second hole, pulling firmly to secure the knot.

D – Inner Side
(cut 2) 21 x 29 holes

Whipstitch · Whipstitch · Whipstitch

Whipstitch to E.

C – Outer Side
(cut 2) 22 x 25 holes

Whipstitch to A. · Whipstitch to B.

Whipstitch to E.

COLOR KEY: Baby's Angel

Embroidery floss		AMOUNT
	Black	7 yds.
	Gray	7 yds.
	Yellow	7 yds.
	Royal Blue	1 yd.
	Sky Blue	1/2 yd.
	White	1/2 yd.

Iridescent yarn		AMOUNT
	White	14 yds.

Worsted-weight	Nylon Plus™	Need-loft®	YARN AMOUNT
White	#01	#41	70 yds.
Straw	#41	#19	12 yds.
Peach	#46	#47	9 yds.
Pink	#11	#07	2 yds.
Black	#02	#00	1 yd.
Bt. Blue	–	#60	1 yd.

STITCH KEY:
— Backstitch/Straight Stitch
● French Knot
— Inner Side/Front & Back Attachment
— Inner Side/Bottom Attachment

B – Back
(cut 1) 64 x 74 holes

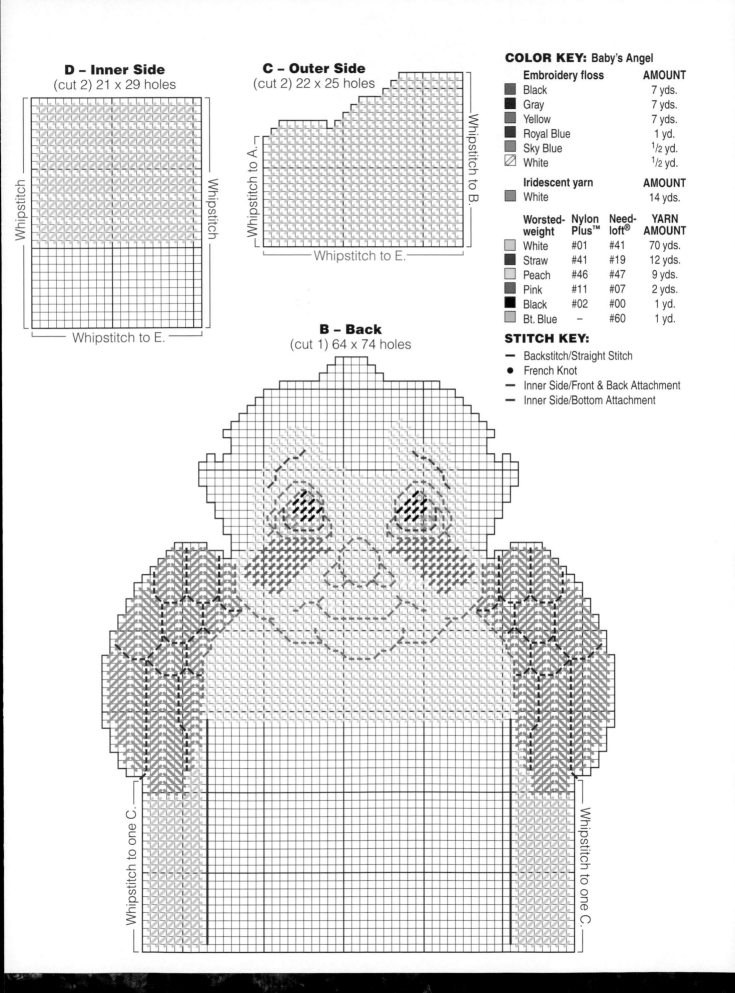

Whipstitch to one C. · Whipstitch to one C.

Snack with the company of your favorite feline friend

Feline Frenzy

SIZE & MATERIALS

Size: Holds an 8 oz. whipped topping bowl.

Materials: Two sheets of 7-count plastic canvas; One 8 oz. whipped topping bowl; Six-strand embroidery floss (for amounts see Color Key); Worsted-weight or plastic canvas yarn (for amounts see Color Key).

INSTRUCTIONS

Cutting Instructions:
(Note: Graphs continued on pages 90 & 91.)
A: For outside cats #1-#5, cut one each according to graphs.
B: For inside cats #1-#5, cut one each according to graph.

C: For base, cut one according to graph.

Stitching Instructions:
1: Using colors and stitches indicated, work pieces according to graphs; with matching colors, Overcast A and B pieces as indicated on graphs.
2: Using six strands floss in colors and embroidery stitches indicated, embroider detail on A and B pieces as indicated.
3: For each cat, holding corresponding A and B pieces wrong sides together, with matching colors, Whipstitch unfinished edges together. Whipstitch and assemble pieces as indicated and according to Cat Bowl Assembly Diagram on page 91.
5: Place bowl into holder, bringing all inner paws over top edge of bowl to hold in place.⊛

COLOR KEY: Feline Frenzy

Embroidery floss		AMOUNT
■	Black	15 yds.
▨	White	2 yds.
■	Baby Green	1/4 yd.
■	Bt. Blue	1/4 yd.
■	Fern	1/4 yd.
□	Lime Green	1/4 yd.
■	Royal	1/4 yd.

Worsted-weight	Nylon Plus™	Need-loft®	YARN AMOUNT
■ Turquoise	#03	#54	16 yds.
▨ Silver	–	#37	15 yds.
□ Eggshell	#24	#39	12 yds.
■ Bittersweet	#18	#52	9 yds.
■ Gray	#23	#38	9 yds.
■ Sandstone	#47	#16	9 yds.
■ Straw	#41	#19	9 yds.
□ White	#01	#41	7 1/2 yds.
▨ Lemon	#25	#20	6 yds.
■ Pink	#11	#07	3 yds.
▨ Black	#02	#00	1 1/2 yds.

STITCH KEY:
- – Backstitch/Straight Stitch
- • French Knot

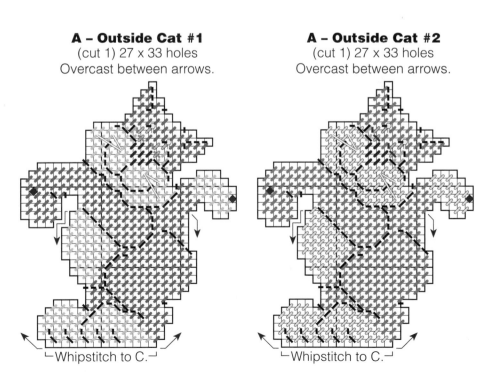

A – Outside Cat #1
(cut 1) 27 x 33 holes
Overcast between arrows.
└Whipstitch to C.┘

A – Outside Cat #2
(cut 1) 27 x 33 holes
Overcast between arrows.
└Whipstitch to C.┘

Feline Frenzy

Instructions & photo on pages 88 & 89.

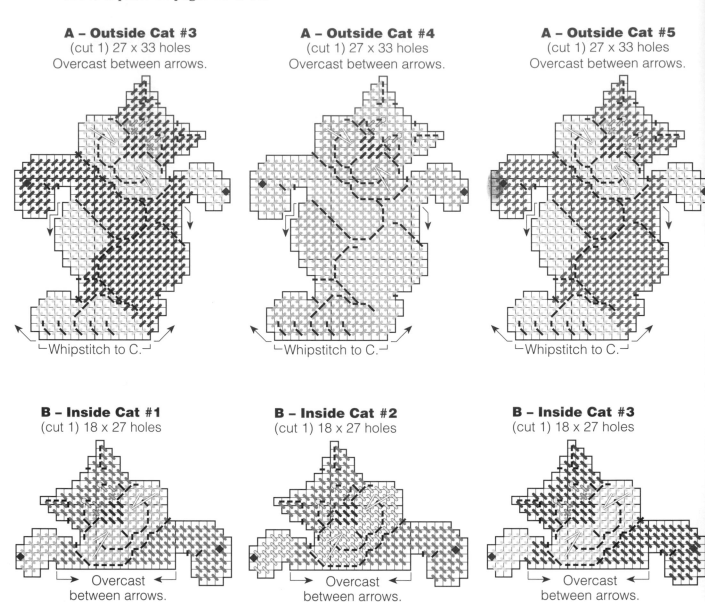

A – Outside Cat #3
(cut 1) 27 x 33 holes
Overcast between arrows.

⌐Whipstitch to C.⌐

A – Outside Cat #4
(cut 1) 27 x 33 holes
Overcast between arrows.

⌐Whipstitch to C.⌐

A – Outside Cat #5
(cut 1) 27 x 33 holes
Overcast between arrows.

⌐Whipstitch to C.⌐

B – Inside Cat #1
(cut 1) 18 x 27 holes

→ Overcast ←
between arrows.

B – Inside Cat #2
(cut 1) 18 x 27 holes

→ Overcast ←
between arrows.

B – Inside Cat #3
(cut 1) 18 x 27 holes

→ Overcast ←
between arrows.

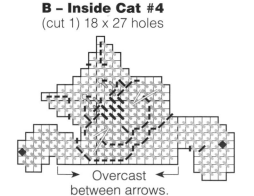

B – Inside Cat #4
(cut 1) 18 x 27 holes

→ Overcast ←
between arrows.

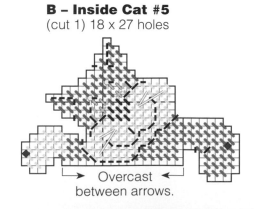

B – Inside Cat #5
(cut 1) 18 x 27 holes

→ Overcast ←
between arrows.

COLOR KEY: Feline Frenzy

Embroidery floss			AMOUNT
■ Black			15 yds.
▨ White			2 yds.
■ Baby Green			1/4 yd.
■ Bt. Blue			1/4 yd.
■ Fern			1/4 yd.
▢ Lime Green			1/4 yd.
■ Royal			1/4 yd.

Worsted-weight	Nylon Plus™	Need-loft®	YARN AMOUNT
■ Turquoise	#03	#54	16 yds.
▢ Silver	–	#37	15 yds.
▢ Eggshell	#24	#39	12 yds.
■ Bittersweet	#18	#52	9 yds.
■ Gray	#23	#38	9 yds.
■ Sandstone	#47	#16	9 yds.
▢ Straw	#41	#19	9 yds.
▢ White	#01	#41	7 1/2 yds.
▨ Lemon	#25	#20	6 yds.
■ Pink	#11	#07	3 yds.
▨ Black	#02	#00	1 1/2 yds.

STITCH KEY:

— Backstitch/Straight Stitch

• French Knot

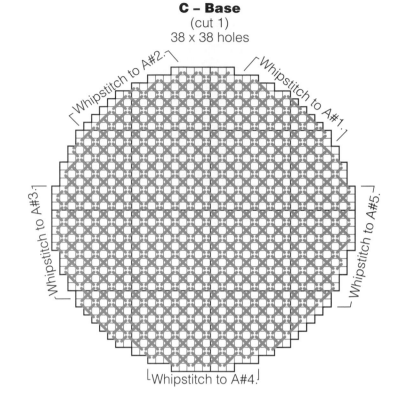

C – Base
(cut 1)
38 x 38 holes

Whipstitch to A#2.
Whipstitch to A#1.
Whipstitch to A#3.
Whipstitch to A#5.
Whipstitch to A#4.

Cat Bowl Assembly Diagram

(Pieces shown in different colors for contrast; gray denotes wrong side.)

Step 1:
With turquoise, Whipstitch bottom edges of A pieces to C, Overcasting unfinished edges of C as you work.

Step 2:
With indicated colors, overlap and tack tails to hands through both thicknesses at ◆ holes.

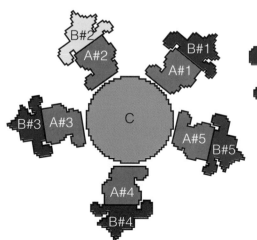

Tack with silver.

Tack with eggshell.

Tack with lemon.

Tack with white.

Step 3:
With eggshell, overlap and tack tail of #5 to hand of #1 through both thicknesses at ◆ holes, forming a complete ring.

Magnificent Magnets

Size & Materials

Sizes: Cool Cat is 4¼" x 4¼"; Top Dog is 3⅞" x 4¼"; Super Star is 3⅞" x 4⅞".

Materials: ½ sheet of 7-count plastic canvas; Three 1" x 1½" magnetic strips; Craft glue or glue gun; Six-strand embroidery floss (for amounts see Color Key on page 99); Worsted-weight or plastic canvas yarn (for amounts see Color Key).

Instructions

Cutting Instructions:
(Note: Graphs on page 99.)
A: For Cool Cat, cut one according to graph.
B: For Top Dog, cut one according to graph.
C: For star, cut one according to graph.
D: For "super" sign, cut one 5 x 17 holes.

Stitching Instructions:
1: Using colors and stitches indicated, work pieces according to graphs; with yellow for star and with matching colors, Overcast pieces.
2: Using six strands floss in colors and embroidery stitches indicated, embroider detail on pieces as indicated on graphs; with white, tack sign to star at ◆ holes.

Bless You Bear

Instructions on next page

Bless You Bear

Photo on page 93.

SIZE & MATERIALS

Size: Bear is 10¼" across x 10⅝" tall, and holds a 3¼" x 4⅝" x 9⅜" box of tissue.

Materials: 1½ sheets of 7-count plastic canvas; Two 1⅛" x 1½" Velcro® closures; Craft glue or glue gun; Six-strand embroidery floss (for amounts see Color Key); Worsted-weight or plastic canvas yarn (for amounts see Color Key).

INSTRUCTIONS

Cutting Instructions:
A: For body, cut one according to graph.
B: For arms, cut two 8 x 32 holes (no graph).
C: For hands, cut two according to graph.
D: For legs, cut two according to graph.
E: For feet, cut two according to graph.
F: For braces #1 and #2, cut two 2 x 11 holes for braces #1 and two 8 x 21 holes for braces #2 (no graphs).

Stitching Instructions:
(Note: F#2 pieces are not worked.)
1: Using colors indicated and Continental Stitch, work A-F#1 (work one D on opposite side of canvas) pieces according to graphs; using six strands floss in colors and embroidery stitches indicated, embroider detail on A, C and E pieces as indicated on graphs.
2: With camel, Whipstitch pieces together as indicated and according to Bear Assembly Illustration; omitting F#2 pieces, Overcast unfinished edges.
3: Place tissue in Bear's lap as shown in photo; glue Velcro® closures to wrong side of hands and top corners of box.✺

A – Body
(cut 1) 36 x 69 holes

Whipstitch to one B.

Whipstitch to one B.

Whipstitch to one F#1.

Whipstitch to one F#1.

Whipstitch to one D.

Whipstitch to one D.

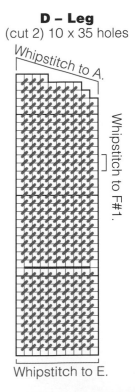

D – Leg
(cut 2) 10 x 35 holes

Whipstitch to A.

Whipstitch to F#1.

Whipstitch to E.

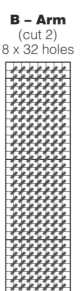

B – Arm
(cut 2)
8 x 32 holes

C – Hand
(cut 2) 14 x 16 holes

Whipstitch to B.

E – Foot
(cut 2) 24 x 24 holes

Whipstitch to D.

Bear Assembly Illustration

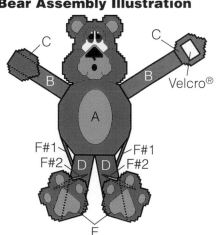

F – Brace #1
(cut 2) 2 x 11 holes

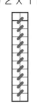

COLOR KEY: Bless You Bear

Embroidery floss			AMOUNT
■ Black			12 yds.
☐ White			1/2 yd.

Worsted-weight	Nylon Plus™	Need-loft®	YARN AMOUNT
■ Camel	#34	#43	60 yds.
■ Beige	#43	#40	16 yds.
■ Black	#02	#00	2 yds.
▨ White	#01	#41	1 yd.
■ Sundown	#16	#10	1/2 yd.

STITCH KEY:
— Backstitch/Straight Stitch
● French Knot
— Brace #2 Attachment

Farm Friends

SIZE & MATERIALS

Sizes: Pig is 6" across x 7⅞" tall, not including paper towel holder; each Coaster Holder is 1⅜" x 4½" x about 1¾" tall.

Materials: 2½ sheets of 7-count plastic canvas; White wrought iron-look up-right paper towel holder; 8" dk. green ⅛" satin ribbon; Six-strand embroidery floss (for amounts see Color Key); Worsted-weight or plastic canvas yarn (for amounts see Color Key).

INSTRUCTIONS

Cutting Instructions:
(Note: Graphs continued on page 98.)
A: For Pig, cut one according to graph.
B: For chicken coasters, cut four according to graph.
C: For chicken holder, cut one according to graph.
D: For cow coasters, cut four according to graph.
E: For cow holder, cut one according to graph.
F: For holder bottoms, cut two 8 x 23 holes (no graph).

Stitching Instructions:
(Note: F pieces are not worked.)
1: Using colors and stitches indicated, work A-E pieces according to graphs; using camel and Rya Knot, randomly work knots (leave ½" loops) on C as indicated on graph. Clip through loops and fluff yarn.
2: With matching colors, omitting bottom edge, Overcast A piece; using six strands black floss and two strands terra cotta and Backstitch, embroider detail on A as indicated.
3: Thread one end of ribbon from front to back through one ◆ hole, then from back to front through adjacent ◆ hole on A as indicated. Pull ends to even and tie into a bow; trim ends. With holly, Whipstitch bottom edge of A to base ring of towel holder as shown in photo.
4: With red for chicken's comb, black yarn for cow's ears and with white, Overcast B and D pieces; with matching colors, Overcast cutout edges of C and E. Using four strands white and six strands black floss and Backstitch, embroider detail on B, D and E pieces as indicated.
5: With camel, Whipstitch C and one F piece together according to Holder Assembly Diagram on page 98; substituting E for C, Whipstitch E and remaining F piece together according to diagram.❋

COLOR KEY: Farm Friends

Embroidery floss			AMOUNT
■ Black			20 yds.
■ Terra Cotta			6 yds.
■ White			2 yds.

Worsted-weight	Nylon Plus™	Need-loft®	YARN AMOUNT
▨ White	#01	#41	48 yds.
▨ Coral	#14	#66	25 yds.
■ Black	#02	#00	18 yds.
■ Camel	#34	#43	15 yds.
▨ Lemon	#25	#20	15 yds.
▨ Xmas Green	#58	#28	10 yds.
■ Pink	#11	#07	8 yds.
▨ Lavender	#12	#05	6 yds.
■ Red	#20	#01	4 yds.
■ Tangerine	#15	#11	4 yds.
▨ Eggshell	#24	#39	3 yds.
□ Holly	#31	#27	1 yd.

STITCH KEY:
- — Backstitch/Straight Stitch
- • French Knot
- □ Rya Knot Area
- ◆ Bow Attachment

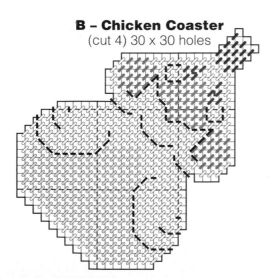

B – Chicken Coaster
(cut 4) 30 x 30 holes

▓ Farm Friends

Instructions & photo on pages 96 & 97.

A – Pig
(cut 1) 39 x 52 holes

C – Chicken Holder
(cut 1) 26 x 29 holes

— Whipstitch to F. —

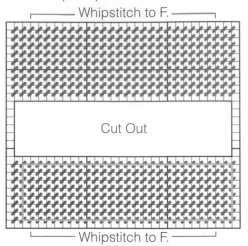

Cut Out

— Whipstitch to F. —

D – Cow Coaster
(cut 4) 33 x 33 holes

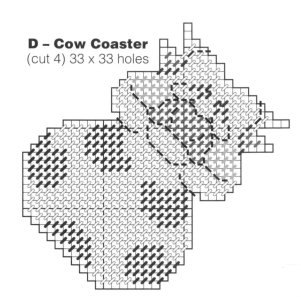

COLOR KEY: Farm Friends

	Embroidery floss			AMOUNT
■	Black			20 yds.
■	Terra Cotta			6 yds.
■	White			2 yds.

	Worsted-weight	Nylon Plus™	Need-loft®	YARN AMOUNT
▨	White	#01	#41	48 yds.
▨	Coral	#14	#66	25 yds.
▨	Black	#02	#00	18 yds.
▨	Camel	#34	#43	15 yds.
▨	Lemon	#25	#20	15 yds.
▨	Xmas Green	#58	#28	10 yds.
▨	Pink	#11	#07	8 yds.
▨	Lavender	#12	#05	6 yds.
■	Red	#20	#01	4 yds.
▨	Tangerine	#15	#11	4 yds.
▨	Eggshell	#24	#39	3 yds.
□	Holly	#31	#27	1 yd.

STITCH KEY:
- — Backstitch/Straight Stitch
- ● French Knot
- ▢ Rya Knot Area
- ◆ Bow Attachment

Holder Assembly Diagram

Step 1:
Whipstitch C and F pieces together.

Step 2:
Overcast unfinished edges of C.

E – Cow Holder
(cut 1) 26 x 29 holes

— Whipstitch to F. —

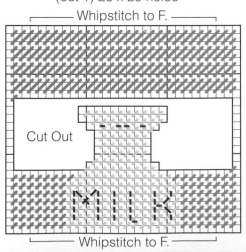

Cut Out

MILK

— Whipstitch to F. —

◼ Magnificient Magnets

Instructions & photo on page 92.

A – Cool Cat
(cut 1) 28 x 28 holes

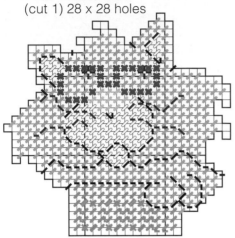

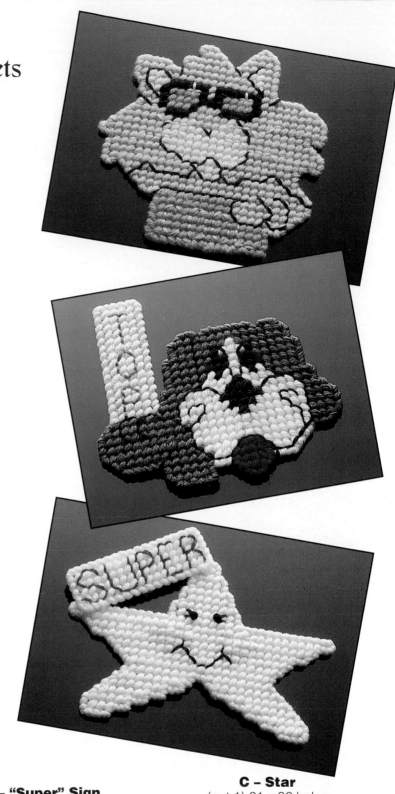

B – Top Dog
(cut 1) 25 x 28 holes

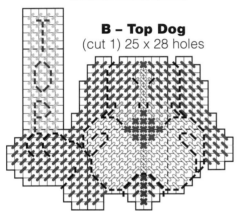

COLOR KEY: Magnificent Magnets

Embroidery floss			AMOUNT
◼ Black			5 yds.
▨ Lt. Green			1 yd.
◼ Red			1 yd.
◼ White			1 yd.
◼ Blue			$1/2$ yd.

Worsted-weight	Nylon Plus™	Need-loft®	YARN AMOUNT
▨ Baby Yellow	#42	#21	6 yds.
▨ Silver	–	#37	6 yds.
◼ Sundown	#16	#10	5 yds.
▨ Eggshell	#24	#39	4 yds.
▨ Baby Blue	#05	#36	3 yds.
◼ Black	#02	#00	$2^1/2$ yds.
▨ Pumpkin	#50	#12	2 yds.
☐ Yellow	#26	#57	2 yds.
▨ White	#01	#41	2 yds.
▨ Baby Pink	#10	#08	1 yd.
▨ Aqua	#60	#51	$1/2$ yd.
▨ Pink	#11	#07	$1/2$ yd.
◼ Red	#20	#01	$1/2$ yd.

STITCH KEY:
- — Backstitch/Straight Stitch
- • French Knot

D – "Super" Sign
(cut 1) 5 x 17 holes

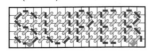

C – Star
(cut 1) 21 x 32 holes

CHAPTER 6

Janelle
Giese

Oregon native Janelle Giese started designing cross-stitch as a hobby in her mid-twenties. Since her mother, Janet, also designed for fun, it was only natural that each of them would begin entering their original stitchery in magazine design contests. An artist from youth, today Janelle designs in counted thread embroidery and plastic canvas. Janet designs in crochet and helps Janelle as a back-up stitcher.

Janelle formed Janelle Marie Designs in 1988 and has been designing as a full-time career since then. Her realistic style, where color combining and highlighting add texture to her diverse projects, is gaining world-wide attention. Working with Kreinik Manufacturing Company, makers of fine metallic and silk threads, Janelle produced two designs that were featured in a book released in England in the autumn of 1998.

Janelle's daughter, Janine, and her husband, Steven, became parents for the first time in April of 1998, when little Julian was born. Now that her daughter has a family of her own, Janelle dreams of traveling around the country. She loves to walk on the beach near her home and also enjoys shopping for antique treasures.

Uncle Sam

SIZE & MATERIALS

Size: 10¼" x 14½".

Materials: One 12" x 18" or larger sheet of 7-count plastic canvas; Six-strand embroidery floss (for amounts see Color Key); ⅛" metallic ribbon or heavy metallic braid (for amount see Color Key); Worsted-weight or plastic canvas yarn (for amounts see Color Key).

INSTRUCTIONS

Cutting Instructions:

For Uncle Sam, cut one according to graph.

Stitching Instructions:

1: Using colors and stitches indicated, work piece according to graph; fill in uncoded areas using navy and Continental Stitch. With black for suit coat, pant edges and hat and with matching colors, Overcast edges.

2: Using six strands floss, ribbon or braid and yarn in colors and stitches indicated, embroider detail as indicated on graph.

3: Hang or display as desired.◉

COLOR KEY: Uncle Sam

Embroidery floss			AMOUNT
■ Black			7 yds.
▨ White			1 yd.

⅛" metallic ribbon or braid	Kreinik		AMOUNT
▨ Gold	#002		5 yds.

Worsted-weight	Nylon Plus™	Need-loft®	YARN AMOUNT
□ Navy	#45	#31	22 yds.
▨ Black	#02	#00	16 yds.
▨ Coral	#14	#66	11 yds.
▨ White	#01	#41	11 yds.
■ Red	#20	#01	7 yds.
▨ Tan	#33	#18	6 yds.
▨ Cerulean	#38	#34	3 yds.
▨ Rose	#52	#06	2 yds.
□ Crimson	#53	#42	1½ yds.

STITCH KEY:
- — Backstitch/Straight Stitch
- × Cross Stitch

Uncle Sam
(cut 1) 67 x 96 holes

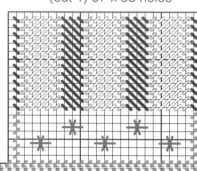

Accent your mantel
with a star-studded
time piece.

Celestial Clock

SIZE & MATERIALS

Size: 2¼" x 8⅝" x about 13" tall.

Materials: Five sheets of clear and four sheets of black 7-count plastic canvas; 2.25" Arabic bezel quartz clock movement; One package of gold seed beads; Gold metallic sewing thread and beading or #9 quilting needle; Fine metallic braid or metallic thread (for amount see Color Key on page 106); Medium and heavy metallic braid or metallic cord (for amounts see Color Key); ⅛" metallic ribbon or metallic yarn (for amount see Color Key); Worsted-weight or plastic canvas yarn (for amounts see Color Key).

INSTRUCTIONS

Cutting Instructions:
(Note: Graphs on pages 106 & 107.)

A: For front pieces, cut two (one from clear and one from black) according to graph.

B: For back pieces, cut two (one from clear and one from black) according to graph.

C: For leg support pieces, cut four (two from clear and two from black) according to graph.

D: For spacers, cut two from clear according to graph.

E: For outer side pieces, from black cut one 12 x 50 holes, one 12 x 82 holes and one 12 x 51 holes (no graphs).

F: For inner side pieces, from black cut one 12 x 46 holes, one 12 x 90 holes and one 12 x 47 holes.

Stitching Instructions:

1: Holding A and one of each color C together at matching edges according to Clock Front Layering Illustration on page 106, using colors indicated and Continental Stitch, work on black canvas side through all thicknesses as one piece according to A graph; holding D pieces to wrong side over matching cutout edges of A pieces and working through all thicknesses as one piece, fill in uncoded areas of front (omit bead cluster attachment areas) using royal dark and Continental Stitch.

2: Using gold metallic braid or cord and Couching Stitch, embroider outlines on A as indicated on graph, securing stitches with gold metallic thread or sewing thread as you work.

3: Using gold metallic braid or cord and Straight Stitch, embroider remaining detail on A as indicated. Using beading or quilting needle and metallic sewing thread, thread and attach five beads at each ▲ hole on front as indicated and according to Bead Cluster Illustration on page 106.

4: Holding B and remaining C pieces together as for front, using colors and stitches indicated, work on black canvas side through all thicknesses according to B graph.

5: Holding E and F pieces end-to-end and together according to Side Layering Illustration on page 107, using colors and stitches indicated, work on outer (E) side through both thicknesses as one piece according to Side Stitch Pattern Guide, working stitches over edges to join seams according to Side Piece Joining Illustration (Note: Illustration shows outer side piece seams only.)

6: With matching colors, Whipstitch cutout edges together on front and back. With black, Whipstitch side assembly to front and back as indicated; Whipstitch unfinished bottom edges together.

7: Attach clock movement in front cutout according to manufacturer's instructions.◉

Celestial Clock

Instructions & photo on pages 104 & 105.

Whipstitch to side assembly between arrows.

Side Stitch Pattern Guide

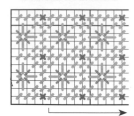

Continue established pattern across each entire piece and over each seam edge.

Side Piece Joining Illustration

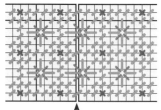

Work pattern across seam edges.

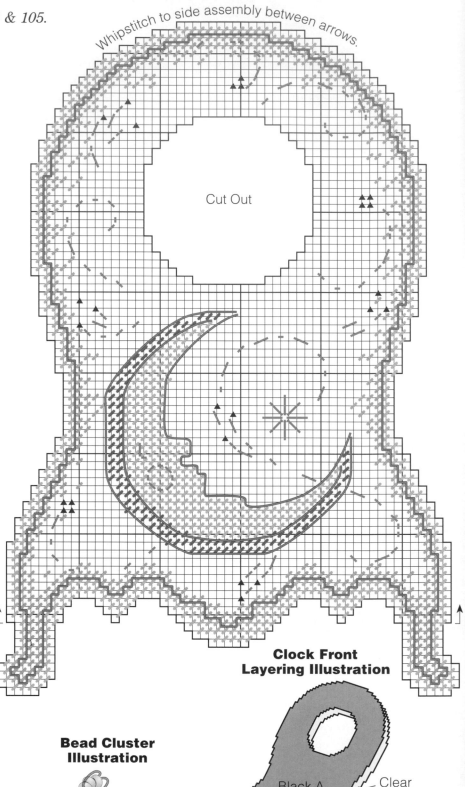

Cut Out

COLOR KEY: Celestial Clock

		Kreinik	AMOUNT
Fine metallic braid or thread			
■ Antique Gold		#205C	20 yds.
Med. metallic braid or cord			
■ Gold		#002HL	7 yds.
Heavy metallic braid or cord			
■ Curry		#2122	14 yds.
1/8" metallic ribbon or metallic yarn			
☐ Antique Gold		#205C	15 yds.

Worsted-weight	Nylon Plus™	Need-loft®	YARN AMOUNT
■ Black	#02	#00	3 oz.
☐ Royal Dark	#07	#48	41 yds.

STITCH KEY:
- — Backstitch/Straight Stitch
- — Couching Stitch
- ▲ Bead Cluster Attachment

Bead Cluster Illustration

Clock Front Layering Illustration

Black A

Clear A

Clear C

Black C

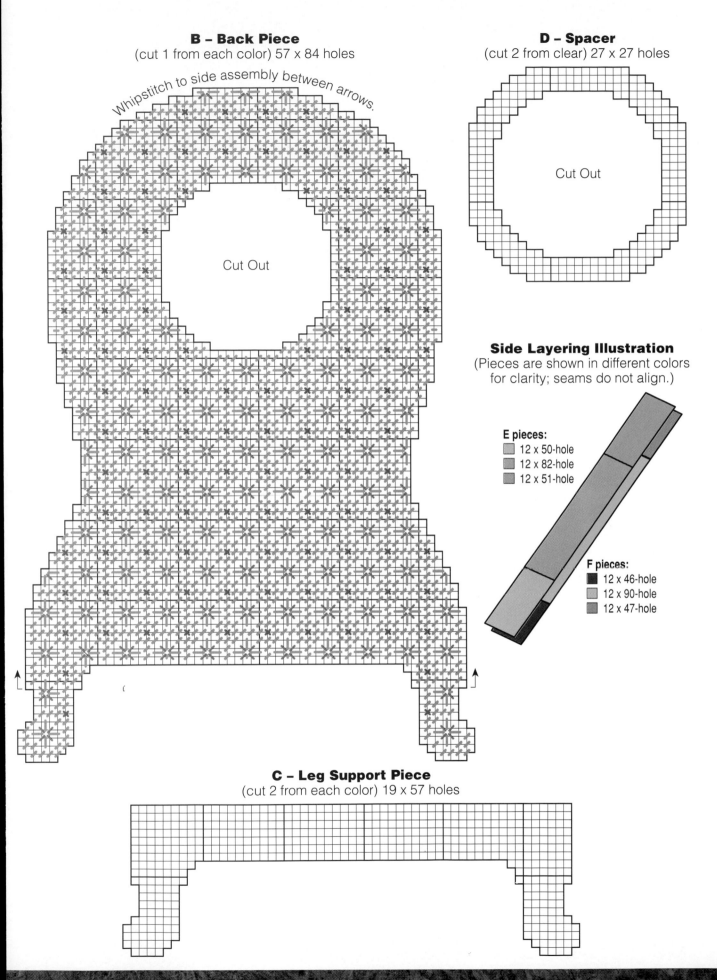

B – Back Piece
(cut 1 from each color) 57 x 84 holes

Whipstitch to side assembly between arrows.

Cut Out

D – Spacer
(cut 2 from clear) 27 x 27 holes

Cut Out

Side Layering Illustration
(Pieces are shown in different colors
for clarity; seams do not align.)

E pieces:
12 x 50-hole
12 x 82-hole
12 x 51-hole

F pieces:
12 x 46-hole
12 x 90-hole
12 x 47-hole

C – Leg Support Piece
(cut 2 from each color) 19 x 57 holes

Kitchen Kitty

SIZE & MATERIALS

Size: 1" x 8½" x 10⅝", not including top hanger.

Materials: Two sheets of 7-count plastic canvas; ⅝" x 1⅜" x 2" "cat" sound effect box; #3 pearl cotton (for amount see Color Key); Six-strand embroidery floss (for amount see Color Key); Worsted-weight or plastic canvas yarn (for amounts see Color Key).

INSTRUCTIONS

Cutting Instructions:
A: For Cat, cut two according to graph.
B: For box support back, cut one 11 x 14 holes (no graph).
C: For box sides, cut two 6 x 14 holes (no graph).
D: For box top and bottom, cut two (one for top and one for bottom) 6 x 11 holes (no graph).

Stitching Instructions:
(Note: B-D pieces are not worked.)
1: Holding A pieces together, using colors indicated and Continental Stitch and omitting stitches within box attachment areas as indicated on graph, work A pieces according to graph

through both thicknesses as one piece; fill in uncoded areas using camel and Continental Stitch. With camel for cat and eggshell for towel holder, Whipstitch edges together.
2: With eggshell, Whipstitch short ends of C and D pieces together (see Holder Assembly Illustration). Holding C and D assembly to indicated area on back of A (see illustration), using colors indicated and Continental Stitch, Whipstitch together, working remaining stitches according to A graph.
3: Using two strands brown floss and Backstitch, embroider whiskers as indicated on graph. Using pearl cotton and embroidery stitches indicated, embroider remaining detail as indicated.
4: Turning sound box so silver button faces wrong side of A, insert box; with eggshell, Whipstitch B to C and D assembly to close.
5: Hang as desired.⊛

Holder Assembly Illustration
(back view)

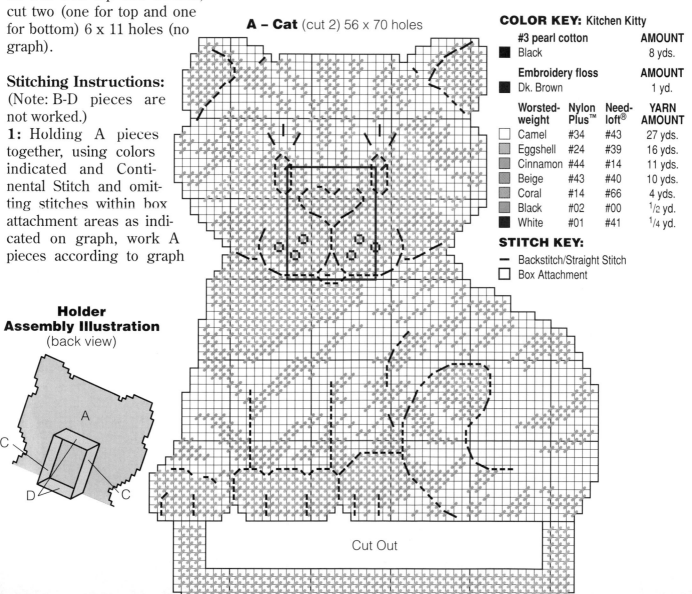

A – Cat (cut 2) 56 x 70 holes

Cut Out

COLOR KEY: Kitchen Kitty

#3 pearl cotton			AMOUNT
■ Black			8 yds.

Embroidery floss			AMOUNT
■ Dk. Brown			1 yd.

Worsted-weight	Nylon Plus™	Need-loft®	YARN AMOUNT
☐ Camel	#34	#43	27 yds.
Eggshell	#24	#39	16 yds.
Cinnamon	#44	#14	11 yds.
Beige	#43	#40	10 yds.
Coral	#14	#66	4 yds.
Black	#02	#00	½ yd.
■ White	#01	#41	¼ yd.

STITCH KEY:
— Backstitch/Straight Stitch
☐ Box Attachment

Let Noah and the gang
help you save for a
rainy day.

110

Rainy Day Savings

SIZE & MATERIALS

Size: 2⅛" x 11⅝" x 8¾" tall.

Materials: Two sheets of 7-count plastic canvas; ⅝" x 1⅞" x 1½"-tall electronic music bank with desired tune; Craft glue or glue gun; Six-strand embroidery floss (for amount see Color Key on page 112); ⅛" metallic ribbon or heavy metallic braid (for amount see Color Key); Wool hair (for amount see Color Key); Worsted-weight or plastic canvas yarn (for amounts see Color Key).

INSTRUCTIONS

Cutting Instructions:
(Note: Graphs on page 112.)

A: For Ark, cut one according to graph.

B: For bank lid top, cut one according to graph.

C: For bank lid lip pieces, cut two 4 x 9 holes and two 4 x 26 holes (no graphs).

D: For bank box sides, cut two 29 x 49 holes (no graph).

E: For bank box ends, cut two 12 x 49 holes (no graph).

F: For bank box bottom, cut one 12 x 29 holes (no graph).

Stitching Instructions:
(Note: C, one D and F pieces are not worked.)

1: Using colors and stitches indicated, work A according to graph; fill in uncoded areas using moss and Continental Stitch. With cinnamon for owl ears, mint for boat ends and with matching colors as shown in photo, Overcast edges.

2: Using ribbon or braid and Cross Stitch, embroider owl eye backgrounds as indicated on graph. Using yarn, wool hair and six strands floss in colors and stitches indicated, embroider remaining detail (work two Straight Stitches for each elephant, Noah and giraffe eye) as indicated.

3: With cinnamon, Whipstitch short ends of C pieces together, forming lid lip (see Lid Assembly Illustration). Holding lid lip centered over one side of B (see Lid Assembly Illustration), using cinnamon and stitches indicated, work B according to graph and through holes on lid lip to join as indicated; Overcast edges of B.

4: Using cinnamon and stitches indicated, work one D and E pieces according to Bank Stitch Pattern Guide. Whipstitch D-F pieces together (see Box Assembly Illustration); Overcast unfinished edges.

5: Matching bottom edges, glue or tack unworked side of bank to center back of A. Slide music bank through cutout on lid and glue in place. Place lid on box.◉

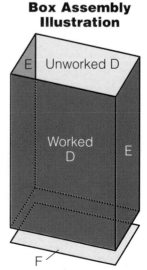

Box Assembly Illustration

E   Unworked D

Worked D   E

F

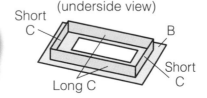

Lid Assembly Illustration
(underside view)

Short C

Long C

B

Short C

Rainy Day Savings

Instructions & photo on pages 110 & 111.

COLOR KEY: Rainy Day Savings

Embroidery floss			AMOUNT
■ Dk. Brown			9 yds.

1/8" metallic ribbon or braid	Kreinik		AMOUNT
☐ Pearl	#032		3 yds.

Wool hair			AMOUNT
▨ White			3 yds.

Worsted-weight	Nylon Plus™	Need-loft®	YARN AMOUNT
■ Cinnamon	#44	#14	63 yds.
■ Mint	#30	#24	7 yds.
☐ Moss	#48	#25	7 yds.
■ Tangerine	#15	#11	5 yds.
▨ Baby Yellow	#42	#21	4 yds.
■ Cerulean	#38	#34	4 yds.
■ Pewter	#40	#65	3 yds.
▨ Baby Blue	#05	#36	2 1/2 yds.
■ Baby Pink	#10	#08	2 yds.
■ Crimson	#53	#42	2 yds.
▨ Maple	#35	#13	2 yds.
■ Black	#02	#00	1 yd.
■ Coral	#14	#66	1 yd.
■ Red	#20	#01	1 yd.
▨ Lavender	#12	#05	1/2 yd.

STITCH KEY:
- — Backstitch/Straight Stitch
- × Cross Stitch
- ☐ Lid Lip Attachment

B – Bank Lid Top (cut 1) 13 x 30 holes

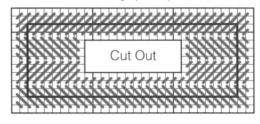

Cut Out

Bank Stitch Pattern Guide

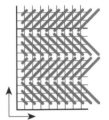

Continue established pattern up and across each entire piece.

A – Ark (cut 1) 57 x 76 holes

Cut out gray areas carefully.

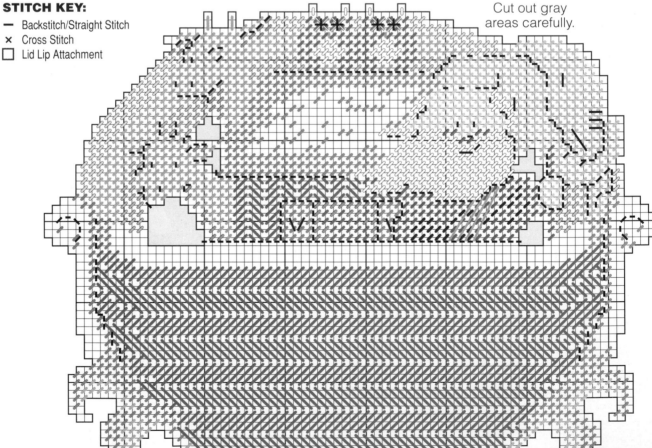

Memo Cottage

Instructions on next page

113

 # Memo Cottage

Photo on page 113.

SIZE & MATERIALS

Size: 1" x 8" x 13¾"; holds a 4⅞" x 8" notepad.

Materials: Two sheets of 7-count plastic canvas; Small silk stemmed posies in desired colors; Craft glue or glue gun; #3 pearl cotton or six-strand embroidery floss (for amount see Color Key); ⅛" metallic ribbon or heavy metallic braid (for amounts see Color Key); Worsted-weight or plastic canvas yarn (for amounts see Color Key).

INSTRUCTIONS

Cutting Instructions:

A: For back, cut one according to graph.

B: For window frame, cut one according to graph.

C: For large roof front, cut one according to graph.

D: For large roof top, cut one 3 x 76 holes (no graph).

E: For entrance front, cut one according to graph.

F: For entrance roof front, cut one according to graph.

G: For entrance roof top, cut one 6 x 36 holes (no graph).

H: For entrance sides, cut two 4 x 21 holes (no graph).

I: For entrance porch sides, cut two 4 x 4 holes (no graph).

J: For window box fronts, cut two 5 x 15 holes.

K: For window box sides, cut four 3 x 5 holes (no graph).

L: For window box bottoms, cut two 3 x 15 holes (no graph).

Stitching Instructions:

1: Positioning B on A as indicated on graph, using sandstone and stitches indicated, work shutter areas through both thicknesses according to A graph; fill in uncoded window frame area using eggshell and Continental Stitch.

2: Using aqua and Continental Stitch, work pencil tab area of A according to graph; bending unworked area of tab to back and working through both thicknesses at tab area to join, using colors and stitches indicated and leaving indicated areas un-

worked, work remainder of A according to graph. Omitting attachment areas, with aqua for cutout and with matching colors, Overcast edges.

3: Using colors and stitches indicated, work C, E and F pieces according to graphs. Using eggshell and Continental Stitch, work D, G and J-L pieces. Using orchid for entrance sides, gray for entrance porch sides and Continental Stitch, work H and I pieces.

4: With eggshell and gray (see photo), Overcast cutout edges of E. Omitting attachment edges, with

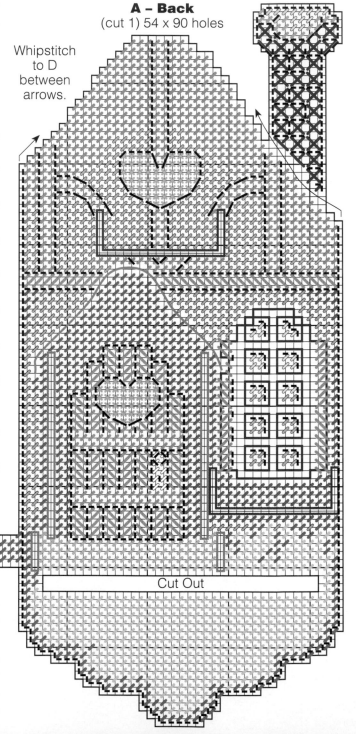

Whipstitch to D between arrows.

A – Back
(cut 1) 54 x 90 holes

Lap Behind

Pencil Tab

Cut Out

eggshell, Overcast C and F pieces.

5: Using yarn and pearl cotton or six strands floss in colors and embroidery stitches indicated, embroider detail on A, C, E, F and J pieces as indicated.

6: Whipstitch pieces together as indicated and according to Cottage Assembly Diagram.

7: Arrange and glue posies inside window boxes as shown in photo. Hang as desired.❁

COLOR KEY: Memo Cottage

#3 pearl cotton or floss			AMOUNT
■ Black			18 yds.

1/8" metallic ribbon or braid		Kreinik	AMOUNT
▨ Pale Yellow		#191	6 yds.
▨ Sunlight		#9100	5 yds.
▨ Blossom		#9200	2 yds.

Worsted-weight	Nylon Plus™	Need-loft®	YARN AMOUNT
▨ Eggshell	#24	#39	24 yds.
▨ Sandstone	#47	#16	13 yds.
▨ Pink	#11	#07	10 yds.
▨ Lilac	#22	#45	9 yds.
▨ Aqua	#60	#51	7 yds.
▨ Aqua Light	#39	#49	7 yds.
▨ Baby Blue	#05	#36	5 yds.
▨ Cerulean	#38	#34	5 yds.
▨ Gray	#23	#38	4 yds.
▨ Baby Pink	#10	#08	3 yds.
■ Coral	#14	#66	3 yds.

STITCH KEY:
- — Backstitch/Straight Stitch
- ☐ Window Frame Attachment
- ☐ Unworked Area/Window Box Attachment
- ☐ Unworked Area/Entrance Attachment
- — Unworked Area/Entrance Roof Attachment

E – Entrance Front
(cut 1) 23 x 37 holes

Whipstitch to one H.

Whipstitch to one H.

Cut Out

Whipstitch to one I.

Whipstitch to one I.

Whipstitch to D between arrows.

C – Large Roof Front
(cut 1)
31 x 51 holes

Cut Out

J – Window Box Front
(cut 2) 5 x 15 holes

B – Window Frame
(cut 1) 13 x 21 holes

Cut out gray areas carefully.

Whipstitch to G between arrows.

F – Entrance Roof Front
(cut 1)
14 x 23 holes

Cottage Assembly Diagram
(Pieces are shown in different colors for contrast.)

Step 1:
For house roof, with eggshell, Whipstitch C and D pieces together and to right side of A; Overcast ends of D.

Step 2:
With matching colors, Whipstitch E, H and I pieces together; omitting attachment edges, Overcast unfinished edges.

C   D

A

Step 3:
Whipstitch H and I pieces to A.

A

E

H

I

Step 4:
For entrance roof, with eggshell, Whipstitch F and G pieces together, and Overcast unfinished short edges of G; Whipstitch G to A.

F   G

A

K

L

Step 5:
For each window box, with eggshell, whipstitch one J, two K and one L together; omitting attachment edges, Overcast unfinished edges.

Step 6:
With pink, Whipstitch window boxes (top box not shown) to A.

CHAPTER 7

Robin Petrina

Transforming plastic canvas into exciting designs is just one of Robin Petrina's talents. When she first began stitching on plastic canvas in 1993, she had no idea her design career would take off so dramatically. Hungry for more than the already-published designs she found, Robin began to create her own projects, and the ideas just kept coming.

Robin understands that today's plastic canvas enthusiasts are very short on leisure time. From her experience as full-time caretaker of two young nephews, Robin tries to create items that are simple and quick to stitch. She loves to design with the holidays in mind, and many of her most popular projects feature seasonal themes. One secret to the versatility of her style is that with a few changes in color and a different style of hat, we can easily transform one of Robin's snowmen, say, into a leprechaun.

Manager of the crafts department in a retail store, Robin has dreams of someday owning her own craft shop. Residing in southwest Pennsylvania with her family, her hobbies include painting, plaster crafts and reading.

Silver Bells

SIZE & MATERIALS

Size: 6¼" across x 12¾", not including hanger.

Materials: Two sheets of 7-count plastic canvas; 1 yd. red ⁵⁄₁₆" braided satin cord; Nine red ½" tinsel pom-poms; Craft glue or glue gun; Metallic cord (for amounts see Color Key).

INSTRUCTIONS

Cutting Instructions:
A: For large bell sides, cut six according to graph.
B: For medium bell sides, cut six according to graph.
C: For small bell sides, cut six according to graph.
D: For holly leaves, cut six according to graph.

Stitching Instructions:
1: Using colors and stitches indicated, work pieces according to graphs; with green/silver, Overcast edges of D pieces.
2: Whipstitch and assemble A-C pieces and braided cord according to Silver Bells Assembly Diagram.
3: Glue two holly leaves and three pom-poms to each Bell as shown in photo.◉

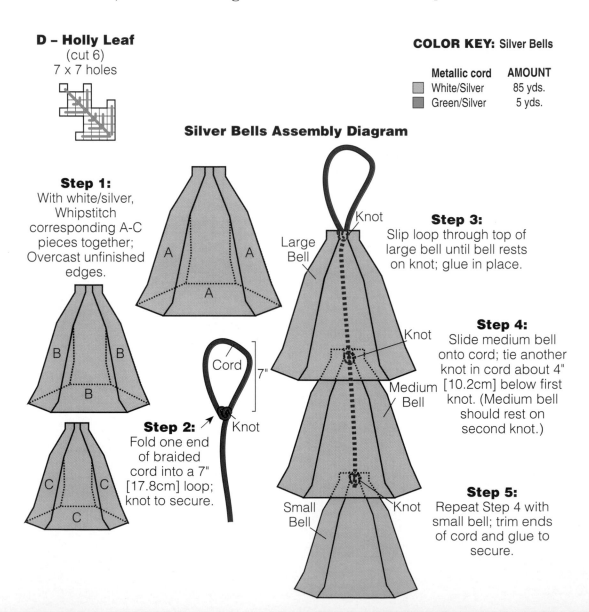

D – Holly Leaf
(cut 6)
7 x 7 holes

COLOR KEY: Silver Bells

Metallic cord	AMOUNT
☐ White/Silver	85 yds.
☐ Green/Silver	5 yds.

Silver Bells Assembly Diagram

Step 1:
With white/silver, Whipstitch corresponding A-C pieces together; Overcast unfinished edges.

Step 2:
Fold one end of braided cord into a 7" [17.8cm] loop; knot to secure.

Step 3:
Slip loop through top of large bell until bell rests on knot; glue in place.

Step 4:
Slide medium bell onto cord; tie another knot in cord about 4" [10.2cm] below first knot. (Medium bell should rest on second knot.)

Step 5:
Repeat Step 4 with small bell; trim ends of cord and glue to secure.

A – Large Bell Side
(cut 6) 22 x 36 holes

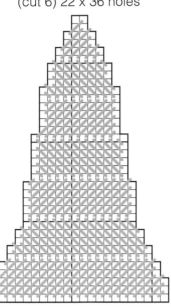

B – Medium Bell Side
(cut 6) 20 x 30 holes

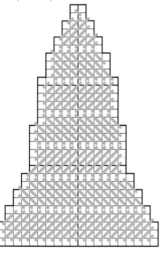

C – Small Bell Side
(cut 6)
18 x 24 holes

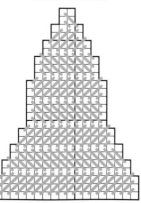

Scare up Halloween treats with this fun-to-stitch centerpiece.

Scary Tree Dish

SIZE & MATERIALS

Size: 8⅜" x 10" x about 9½" tall.
Materials: 3½ sheets of clear 7-count plastic canvas; Scraps of black 7-count plastic canvas; Craft glue or glue gun; Worsted-weight or plastic canvas yarn (for amounts see Color Key on page 123).

INSTRUCTIONS

Cutting Instructions:
(Notes: Graphs on pages 122 & 123. Use black for N and clear canvas for remaining pieces.)
A: For base bottom pieces, cut two from clear 55 x 66 holes (no graph).
B: For base long sides, cut two according to graph.
C: For base short sides, cut two according to graph.
D: For tree pieces #1, cut two according to graph.
E: For tree pieces #2, cut three according to graph.
F: For tree pieces #3, cut three according to graph.
G: For branches #1 and #2, cut one each according to graphs.
H: For eyes #1 and #2, cut one each according to graphs.

I: For large ghost, cut one according to graph.
J: For small ghost, cut one according to graph.
K: For pumpkins, cut two according to graph.
L: For sign, cut one according to graph.
M: For post, cut one 3 x 21 holes.
N: For spiders, cut two according to graph.

Stitching Instructions:
(Note: One A piece is not worked.)
1: Using colors and stitches indicated, work one A and B-N (one D on opposite side of canvas) pieces according to graphs and stitch pattern guide. With black for eyes, forest for pumpkin stems and with matching colors, Overcast edges of H-N (Omit legs on spiders.) pieces; with cinnamon, Overcast D-F (Omit Whipstitch edges.) and G pieces.
2: Using colors (Separate yarn into individual plies, if desired.) and embroidery stitches indicated, embroider detail on H-J, L and N pieces as indicated on graphs.
3: For tree, with brown, Whipstitch D-F pieces together as indicated and according to Tree Assembly Illustration on page 123.
4: Whipstitch and assemble A-C pieces and tree according to Dish Assembly Diagram.
5: Glue branches, eyes, one pumpkin and ghosts to tree as shown in photo. Glue sign to post; glue remaining pumpkin, post and spiders to Dish as shown.◉

COLOR KEY: Scary Tree Dish

	Worsted-weight	Nylon Plus™	Need-loft®	YARN AMOUNT
■	Cinnamon	#44	#14	62 yds.
☐	Silver	–	#37	56 yds.
■	Forest	#32	#29	40 yds.
☐	White	#01	#41	15 yds.
■	Bittersweet	#18	#52	7 yds.
■	Black	#02	#00	6 yds.
■	Camel	#34	#43	6 yds.

STITCH KEY:
— Backstitch/Straight Stitch
● French Knot
× Cross Stitch

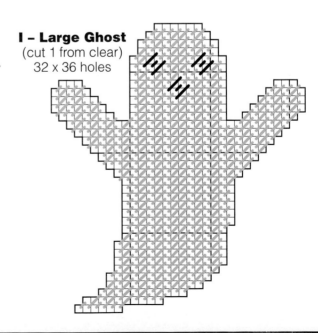

I – Large Ghost
(cut 1 from clear)
32 x 36 holes

Scary Tree Dish

Instructions & photo on pages 120 & 121.

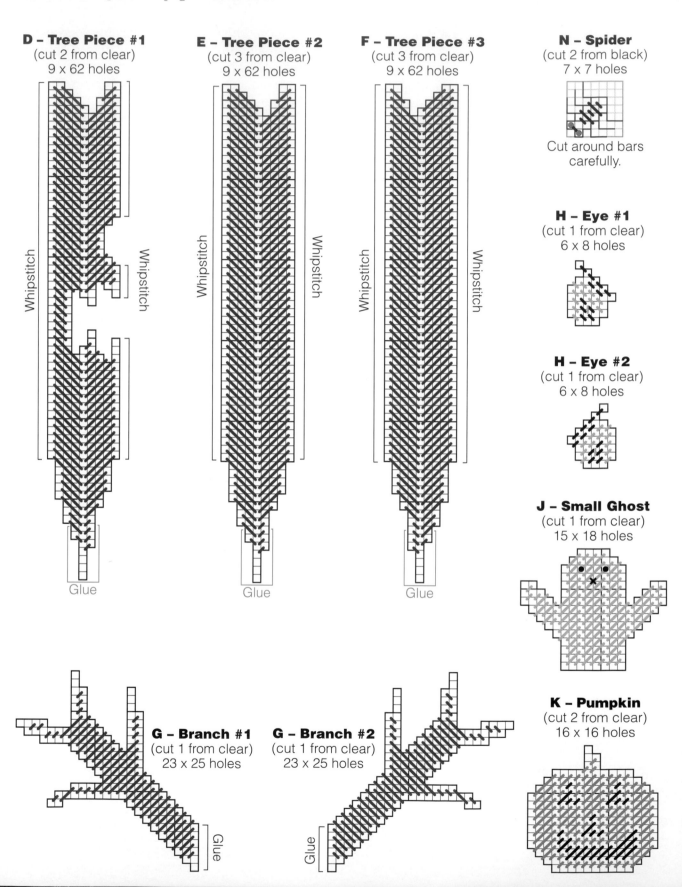

D – Tree Piece #1
(cut 2 from clear)
9 x 62 holes

Whipstitch

Whipstitch

Glue

E – Tree Piece #2
(cut 3 from clear)
9 x 62 holes

Whipstitch

Whipstitch

Glue

F – Tree Piece #3
(cut 3 from clear)
9 x 62 holes

Whipstitch

Whipstitch

Glue

N – Spider
(cut 2 from black)
7 x 7 holes

Cut around bars
carefully.

H – Eye #1
(cut 1 from clear)
6 x 8 holes

H – Eye #2
(cut 1 from clear)
6 x 8 holes

J – Small Ghost
(cut 1 from clear)
15 x 18 holes

K – Pumpkin
(cut 2 from clear)
16 x 16 holes

G – Branch #1
(cut 1 from clear)
23 x 25 holes

Glue

G – Branch #2
(cut 1 from clear)
23 x 25 holes

Glue

B – Base Long Side
(cut 2 from clear) 15 x 66 holes

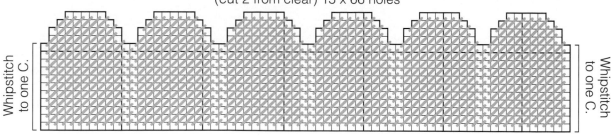

Whipstitch to one C.

Whipstitch to one C.

C – Base Short Side
(cut 2 from clear) 15 x 55 holes

Whipstitch to one B.

Whipstitch to one B.

M – Post
(cut 1 from clear)
3 x 21 holes

L – Sign
(cut 1 from clear) 8 x 24 holes

HAPPY HAUNTING

Base Stitch Pattern Guide

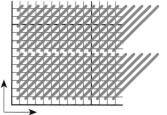

Continue established pattern up and across entire piece.

Tree Assembly Illustration
(Pieces are shown in different colors for contrast.)

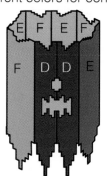

E F E F
F D D E

COLOR KEY: Scary Tree Dish

	Worsted-weight	Nylon Plus™	Need-loft®	YARN AMOUNT
■	Cinnamon	#44	#14	62 yds.
□	Silver	–	#37	56 yds.
▨	Forest	#32	#29	40 yds.
□	White	#01	#41	15 yds.
▨	Bittersweet	#18	#52	7 yds.
■	Black	#02	#00	6 yds.
▨	Camel	#34	#43	6 yds.

STITCH KEY:
- — Backstitch/Straight Stitch
- ● French Knot
- ✕ Cross Stitch

Dish Assembly Diagram
(Pieces are shown in different colors for contrast.)

Step 1:
With right side of worked A facing up, with silver, Whipstitch A-C pieces together through all thicknesses.

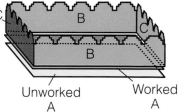

C B C
B
Unworked A   Worked A

Step 2:
Center tree inside Dish and glue indicated edges to base.

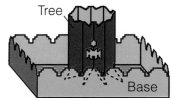

Tree
Base

Starlit Tree Box

SIZE & MATERIALS

Size: 6¾" x 7¼" x 1¾" tall.

Materials: 1½ sheets of 7-count plastic canvas; 1¾ yds. red ⅛" satin ribbon; Craft glue or glue gun; Metallic cord (for amount see Color Key); Worsted-weight or plastic canvas yarn (for amount see Color Key).

INSTRUCTIONS

Cutting Instructions:

A: For lid top, cut one according to graph..

B: For lid side pieces, cut two 2 x 21 holes, one 2 x 17 holes, four 2 x 15 holes, two 2 x 14 holes and six 2 x 6 holes (no graphs).

C: For box bottom, cut one according to graph.

D: For box sides, cut two 10 x 17 holes, two 10 x 16 holes, one 10 x 15 holes, two 10 x 14 holes, two 10 x 13 holes and six 6 x 10 holes (no graphs).

Stitching Instructions:

(Note: C piece is not worked.)

1: Using white and stitches indicated, work A, B and D pieces according to graph and stitch pattern guides.

2: Using cord and embroidery stitches indicated, embroider detail on A as indicated on graph.

3: With white, Whipstitch A and B pieces together according to Lid Assembly Illustration; with cord, Overcast unfinished edges. With white, Whipstitch C and D pieces together according to Box Assembly Illustration; Overcast unfinished edges.

(Note: Cut ribbon into seven 9" lengths.)

4: Tie each ribbon into a small bow; trim ends. Glue bows to lid as shown in photo.❂

A – Lid Top
(cut 1) 44 x 47 holes

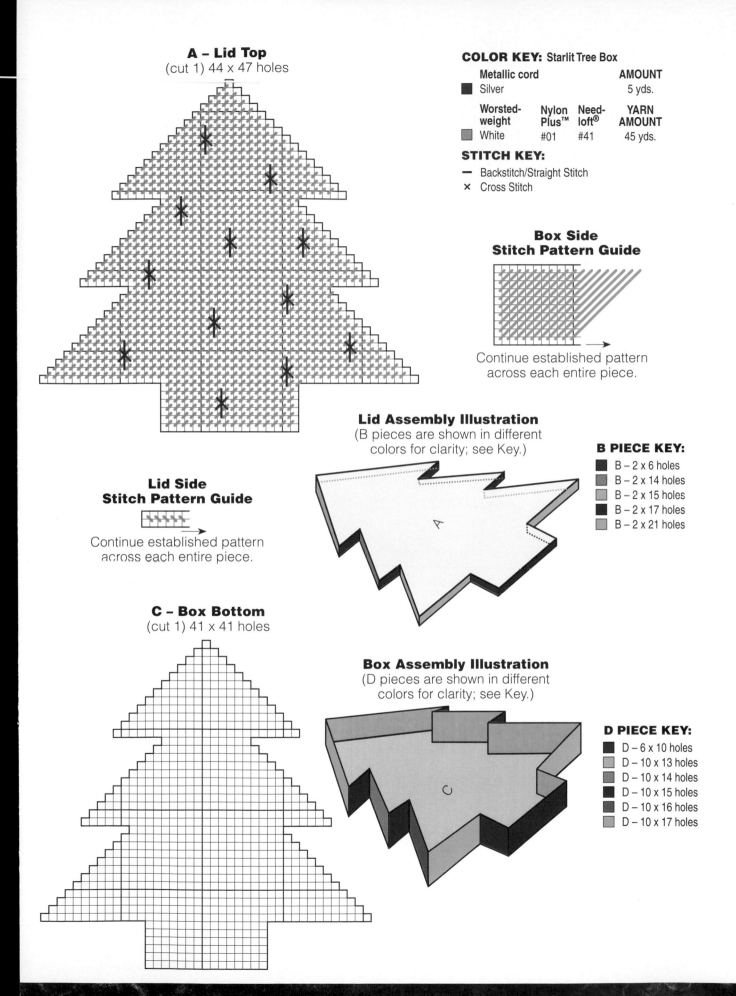

COLOR KEY: Starlit Tree Box

	Metallic cord			AMOUNT
■	Silver			5 yds.

	Worsted-weight	Nylon Plus™	Need-loft®	YARN AMOUNT
■	White	#01	#41	45 yds.

STITCH KEY:
- — Backstitch/Straight Stitch
- × Cross Stitch

Box Side Stitch Pattern Guide
Continue established pattern across each entire piece.

Lid Assembly Illustration
(B pieces are shown in different colors for clarity; see Key.)

B PIECE KEY:
- ■ B – 2 x 6 holes
- ■ B – 2 x 14 holes
- ■ B – 2 x 15 holes
- ■ B – 2 x 17 holes
- ■ B – 2 x 21 holes

Lid Side Stitch Pattern Guide
Continue established pattern across each entire piece.

C – Box Bottom
(cut 1) 41 x 41 holes

Box Assembly Illustration
(D pieces are shown in different colors for clarity; see Key.)

D PIECE KEY:
- ■ D – 6 x 10 holes
- ■ D – 10 x 13 holes
- ■ D – 10 x 14 holes
- ■ D – 10 x 15 holes
- ■ D – 10 x 16 holes
- ■ D – 10 x 17 holes

Tweet Welcome

Let these feathered friends greet guests with a heartfelt welcome.

SIZE & MATERIALS

Size: 7½" x 12¾".

Materials: One sheet of clear 7-count plastic canvas; ¼ sheet of white 7-count plastic canvas; Craft glue or glue gun; Worsted-weight or plastic canvas yarn (for amounts see Color Key).

INSTRUCTIONS

Cutting Instructions:
(Notes: Graphs continued on page 131. Use white for B and clear canvas for remaining pieces.)
A: For sign, cut one according to graph.
B: For fence, cut one according to graph.
C: For birds #1 and #2, cut two each according to graphs.
D: For flowers, cut five according to graph.
E: For letters, cut number needed according to graphs.

Stitching Instructions:
1: Using colors and stitches indicated, work pieces according to graphs; with lemon for birds' beaks, sail blue for letters, peach for flowers, brown for cutout edges of birdhouses and with matching colors, Overcast unfinished edges of A and C-E pieces. (B piece is not Overcast.)
2: Using colors indicated (Separate yarn into individual plies, if desired.) and French Knot, embroider detail on C and D pieces as indicated on graphs.
3: Glue fence to bottom edge of sign; glue letters to clouds, birds to fence and center birdhouse and flowers to fence as shown in photo.
4: Hang or display as desired.◉

COLOR KEY: Tweet Welcome

	Worsted-weight	Nylon Plus™	Need-loft®	YARN AMOUNT
	White	#01	#41	20 yds.
	Camel	#34	#43	15 yds.
	Brown	#36	#15	9 yds.
	Sail Blue	#04	#35	7 yds.
	Fern	#57	#23	4 yds.
	Peach	#46	#47	3 yds.
	Lemon	#25	#20	½ yd.

STITCH KEY:
- ● French Knot

D – Flower
(cut 5 from clear)
3 x 3 holes

A – Sign
(cut 1 from clear) 49 x 81 holes

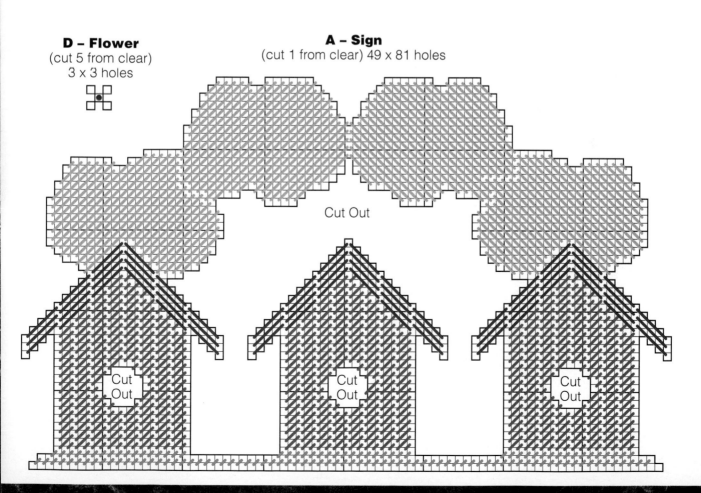

Cut Out

Cut Out

Cut Out

Cut Out

Fill your basket
with sweet treats
or fresh-cut flowers.

128

Pastel Basket

SIZE & MATERIALS

Size: 6¾" across x 5¼" tall, not including handle.
Materials: Two sheets of 7-count plastic canvas; craft glue or glue gun; Worsted-weight or plastic canvas yarn (for amounts see Color Key).

INSTRUCTIONS

Cutting Instructions:
A: For sides, cut six according to graph.
B: For bottom, cut one according to graph.
C: For handle pieces, cut two 3 x 61 holes (no graph).

Stitching Instructions:
(Note: B piece is not worked.)
1: Using colors and stitches indicated, work A pieces according to graph. For handle, overlapping four holes at one end of each piece and working through both thicknesses at overlap area to join, using white and Continental Stitch, work C pieces; Overcast edges.
2: With matching colors as shown in photo, Whipstitch A and B pieces together according to Pastel Basket Assembly Illustration; with white, Overcast unfinished edges.
3: Glue handle ends to inside of Basket.

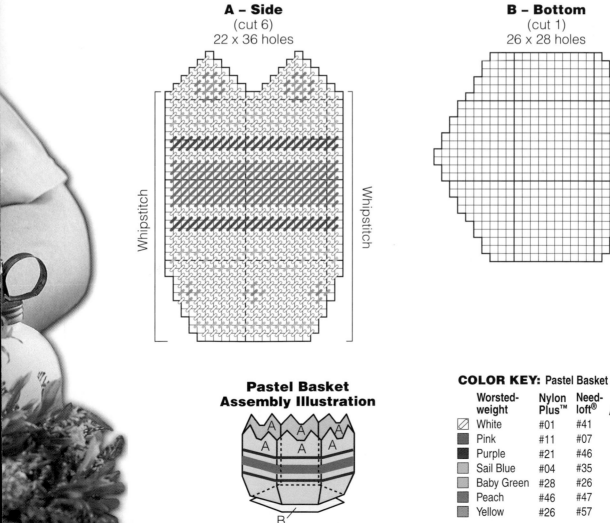

A – Side
(cut 6)
22 x 36 holes

Whipstitch

Whipstitch

B – Bottom
(cut 1)
26 x 28 holes

**Pastel Basket
Assembly Illustration**

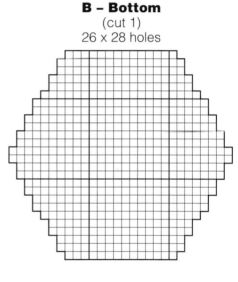

COLOR KEY: Pastel Basket

	Worsted-weight	Nylon Plus™	Need-loft®	YARN AMOUNT
▨	White	#01	#41	60 yds.
■	Pink	#11	#07	12 yds.
■	Purple	#21	#46	8 yds.
▨	Sail Blue	#04	#35	6 yds.
▨	Baby Green	#28	#26	3 yds.
■	Peach	#46	#47	3 yds.
▨	Yellow	#26	#57	3 yds.

Apple Crate

SIZE & MATERIALS

Size: About 8" across x 5⅛" tall.

Materials: 1½ sheets of 7-count plastic canvas; Worsted-weight or plastic canvas yarn (for amounts see Color Key).

INSTRUCTIONS

Cutting Instructions:
A: For sides, cut eight according to graph.

B: For bottom, cut one according to graph.

Stitching Instructions:
(Note: B piece is not worked.)
1: Using colors and stitches indicated, work A pieces according to graph; with crimson for apples, cinnamon for apple stems and with forest, Overcast cutout edges of A pieces.
2: With forest, Whipstitch A and B pieces together according to Apple Crate Assembly Illustration; Overcast unfinished top edges.⊛

COLOR KEY: Apple Crate

Worsted-weight	Nylon Plus™	Need-loft®	YARN AMOUNT
■ Crimson	#53	#42	28 yds.
■ Forest	#32	#29	21 yds.
▧ Beige	#43	#40	10 yds.
□ Cinnamon	#44	#14	2 yds.

A – Side
(cut 8) 21 x 34 holes

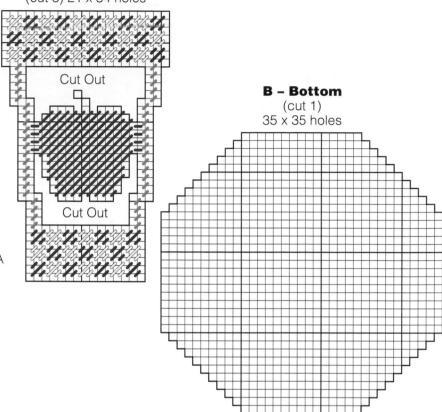

Cut Out

Cut Out

B – Bottom
(cut 1)
35 x 35 holes

Apple Crate Assembly Illustration
(Apple motifs are not shown for clarity.)

A   A   A   A   A
A   A   A
B

■ Tweet Welcome

Instructions & photo on pages 126 & 127.

COLOR KEY: Tweet Welcome

Worsted-weight	Nylon Plus™	Need-loft®	YARN AMOUNT
▨ White	#01	#41	20 yds.
■ Camel	#34	#43	15 yds.
■ Brown	#36	#15	9 yds.
▨ Sail Blue	#04	#35	7 yds.
■ Fern	#57	#23	4 yds.
■ Peach	#46	#47	3 yds.
□ Lemon	#25	#20	1/2 yd.

STITCH KEY:
● French Knot

E – Letter "W"
(cut 1 from clear)
5 x 7 holes

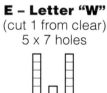

E – Letter "E"
(cut 2 from clear)
5 x 7 holes

E – Letter "L"
(cut 1 from clear)
5 x 7 holes

E – Letter "C"
(cut 1 from clear)
5 x 7 holes

E – Letter "O"
(cut 1 from clear)
5 x 7 holes

Cut out gray area carefully.

E – Letter "M"
(cut 1 from clear)
5 x 7 holes

C – Bird #1
(cut 2 from clear)
9 x 10 holes

C – Bird #2
(cut 2 from clear)
9 x 10 holes

B – Fence
(cut 1 from white) 6 x 77 holes

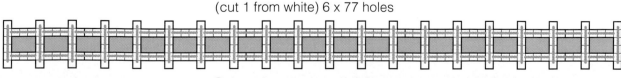

Cut out gray areas carefully.

Mike Vickery

The artistic talent of designer Mike Vickery is shown in fine detail in each of his many popular needlework designs. His love of nature, sports and vivid colors are expressed in each piece, whether communicated as cross stitch or plastic canvas designs. We can almost see Mike, the artist, sitting by a pond or at a ball game, with pens and paper in hand, sketching, mixing and matching colors, focusing on every detail in order to bring the piece to life.

Having his work published by 17 different companies since his debut in the world of needlework in 1992, Mike plans to launch a publishing enterprise of his own. He says that he will continue to freelance his designs, so his patrons are sure to find his work available in many locations. We can also look forward to Mike having his own internet website in the near future.

Mike and his wife, Amy, live in rural Georgia with their two children, Megan and Justin. Mike enjoys music, gardening, jogging and being involved with his children in baseball and scouting.

Christmas Train

SIZE & MATERIALS

Sizes: Engine is 3¾" x 13½" x 6½" tall; Boxcar is 3¾" x 11" x 6¼" tall; Caboose is 3¾" x 11" x 6⅞" tall.

Materials: Four sheets of 7-count plastic canvas; Craft glue or glue gun; Worsted-weight or plastic canvas yarn (for amounts see Color Key on page 137).

INSTRUCTIONS

Cutting Instructions:
(Note: Graphs on pages 136 & 137.)
A: For Engine, cut one according to graph.
B: For Boxcar, cut one according to graph.
C: For Caboose, cut one according to graph.
D: For box front, back and bottoms, cut nine 22 x 52 holes (no graph).

Hold greeting cards or Christmas treats in each car of Santa's express.

E: For box ends, cut six 22 x 22 holes (no graph).

Stitching Instructions:
(Note: Three D pieces are not worked for bottoms.)
1: Using colors and stitches indicated, work A-C pieces according to graphs; with matching colors as shown in photo, Overcast unfinished edges.

2: Using black and French knot, embroider detail on A piece as indicated on graph.
3: Using gray and Long Stitch, work six D and E pieces according to Box Stitch Pattern Guide; for each box (make 3), assemble according to Box Assembly Illustration on page 137.
4: Matching bottom edges, glue one train piece to one long side of each box. Display as desired.◉

Christmas Train

Instructions on pages 134 & 135.

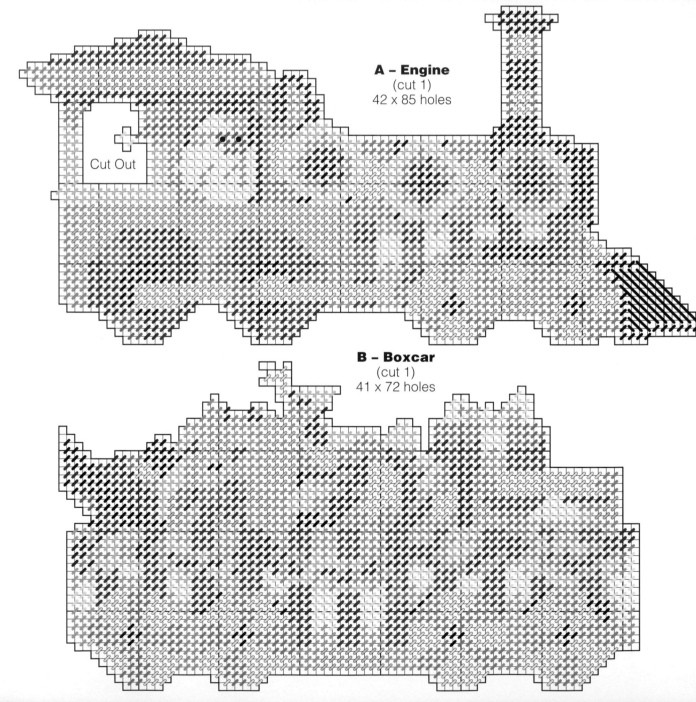

A – Engine
(cut 1)
42 x 85 holes

Cut Out

B – Boxcar
(cut 1)
41 x 72 holes

C – Caboose
(cut 1)
45 x 73 holes

Box Assembly Illustration

Worked D
Worked D
E
E
Unworked D

Box Stitch Pattern Guide

Continue established pattern across entire piece.

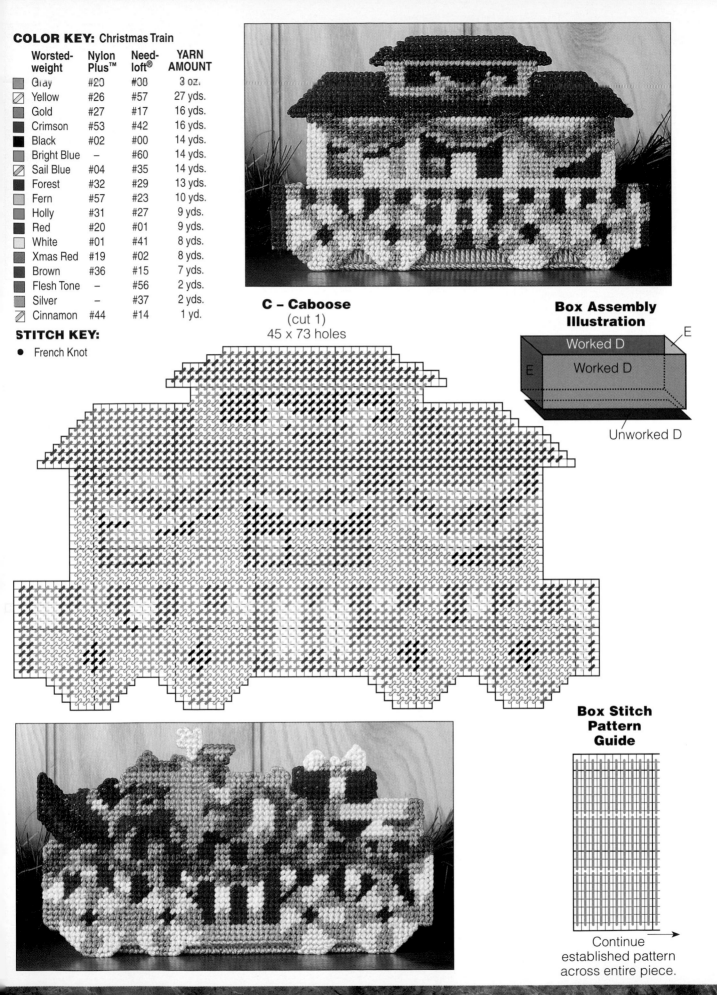

Tropical Fish Coasters

SIZE & MATERIALS

Sizes: From 5½" x 6" to 4½" x 7".

Materials: One sheet of 7-count plastic canvas; Worsted-weight or plastic canvas yarn (for amounts see Color Key).

INSTRUCTIONS

Cutting Instructions:
For Fish #1-#4, cut one each according to graphs.

Stitching Instructions:
1: Using colors and stitches indicated, work pieces according to graphs; with black for Fish #1, yellow for Fish #2, gold for Fish #3 and cinnamon for Fish #4, Overcast unfinished edges.
2: Using colors and embroidery stitches indicated, embroider detail as indicated on graphs.❂

B – Fish #2
(cut 1)
30 x 41 holes

A – Fish #1
(cut 1)
35 x 40 holes

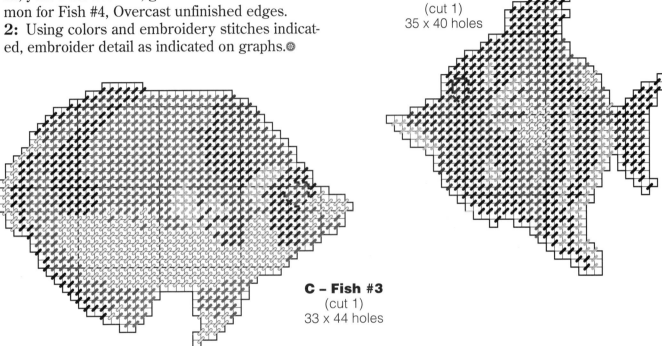

C – Fish #3
(cut 1)
33 x 44 holes

D – Fish #4
(cut 1)
29 x 46 holes

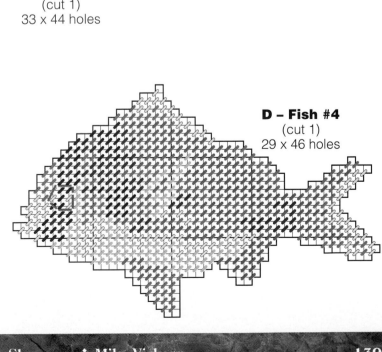

COLOR KEY: Tropical Fish Coasters

	Worsted-weight	Nylon Plus™	Need-loft®	YARN AMOUNT
▨	Yellow	#26	#57	18 yds.
■	Black	#02	#00	16 yds.
▨	Gold	#27	#17	12 yds.
▨	Pumpkin	#50	#12	11 yds.
▨	Cinnamon	#44	#14	6 yds.
▨	White	#01	#41	6 yds.
▨	Gray	#23	#38	5 yds.
▨	Sundown	#16	#10	4 yds.
▨	Sail Blue	#04	#35	3 yds.
■	Bt. Blue	–	#60	2 yds.

STITCH KEY:
— Backstitch/Straight Stitch

Display precious
first photos of Santa
and baby.

Santa & Me Frame

SIZE & MATERIALS

Size: 8½" x 13⅝", with a 5" x 5¼" photo window.

Materials: Two sheets of 7-count plastic canvas; ⅓ yd. yellow ⅝" grosgrain ribbon; Craft glue or glue gun; Worsted-weight or plastic canvas yarn (for amounts see Color Key).

INSTRUCTIONS

Cutting Instructions:

A: For front, cut one according to graph.
B: For backing, cut one 56 x 90 holes (no graph).

Stitching Instructions:

(Note: B piece is not worked.)
1: Using colors and stitches indicated, work A piece according to graph; fill in uncoded areas using baby blue and Continental Stitch; with black, Overcast cutout edges.
2: Tie ribbon into a bow and glue to front as indicated on graph.
3: Center photo over cutout on wrong side; glue at top and bottom to secure.
4: Holding B to wrong side of A, with baby blue, Whipstitch together as indicated; Overcast unfinished edges of front. Hang or display as desired.✿

STITCH KEY:
✦ Bow Attachment

A – Front
(cut 1)
56 x 90 holes

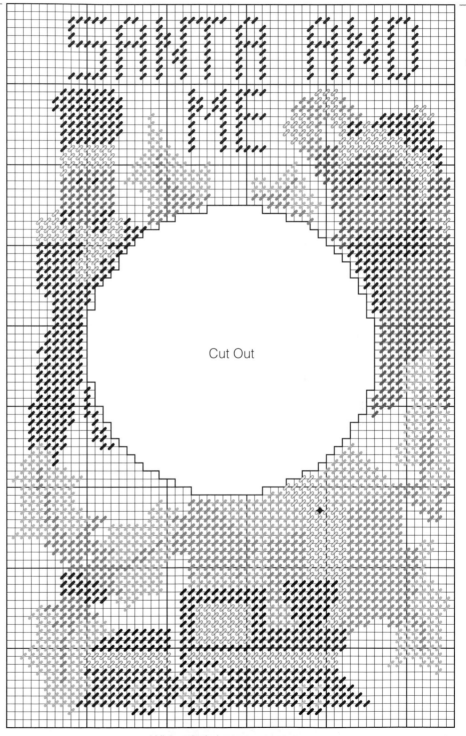

Cut Out

Whipstitch between arrows.

COLOR KEY: Santa & Me Frame

Worsted-weight	Nylon Plus™	Need-loft®	YARN AMOUNT
☐ Baby Blue	#05	#36	96 yds.
■ Red	#20	#01	18 yds.
■ Fern	#57	#23	16 yds.
■ Cinnamon	#44	#14	14 yds.
◪ Yellow	#26	#57	13 yds.
■ Bt. Blue	–	#60	10 yds.
■ Black	#02	#00	9 yds.
■ Holly	#31	#27	8 yds.
■ Royal	#09	#32	7 yds.
■ Crimson	#53	#42	5 yds.
■ Camel	#34	#43	3 yds.
■ Pink	#11	#07	2 yds.
◪ White	#01	#41	2 yds.
■ Xmas Red	#19	#02	2 yds.
■ Gray	#23	#38	1 yd.

Pansies Door Hanger

SIZE & MATERIALS

Size: 5¾" x 14⅜".

Materials: One 12" x 18" or larger sheet of 7-count plastic canvas; Worsted-weight or plastic canvas yarn (for amounts see Color Key).

INSTRUCTIONS

Cutting Instructions:
For Door Hanger, cut one according to graph.

Stitching Instructions:
1: Using colors and stitches indicated, work according to graph; with burgundy, Overcast unfinished edges.
2: Using red and Backstitch, embroider detail as indicated on graph; hang as desired.❀

COLOR KEY: Pansies Door Hanger

	Worsted-weight	Nylon Plus™	Need-loft®	YARN AMOUNT
■	Burgundy	#13	#03	20 yds.
■	Gold	#27	#17	18 yds.
■	Red	#20	#01	11 yds.
▢	White	#01	#41	9 yds.
■	Forest	#32	#29	7 yds.
■	Baby Blue	#05	#36	6 yds.
■	Brown	#36	#15	4 yds.
■	Holly	#31	#27	4 yds.
■	Lilac	#22	#45	4 yds.
▨	Yellow	#26	#57	3 yds.
■	Fern	#57	#23	2 yds.
■	Purple	#21	#46	2 yds.

STITCH KEY:
— Backstitch/Straight Stitch

Pansies Door Hanger
(cut 1)
37 x 95 holes

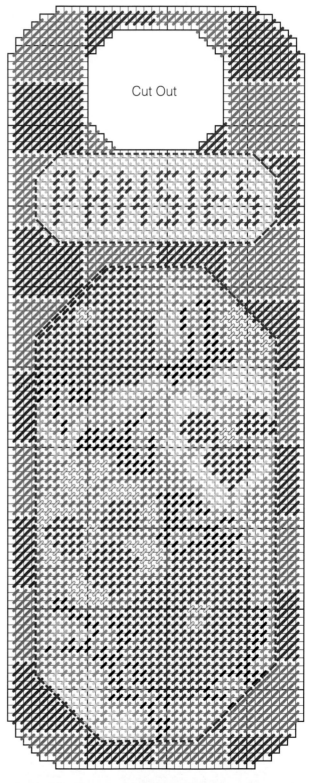

Cut Out

Sunny Sunflowers

Instructions on page 146

Add a touch of nature's brilliance with majestic sunflower accents.

Sunny Sunflowers

Photo on pages 144 & 145.

SIZE & MATERIALS

Sizes: Sunflower Picture is 7¾" x 15"; Magazine Box is 8½" x 11½" x 13¾" tall; Vase is 6⅜" square x 13¾" tall.

Materials: Seven 12" x 18" or larger sheets of 7-count plastic canvas; Worsted-weight or plastic canvas yarn (for amounts see Color Key).

INSTRUCTIONS

Cutting Instructions:
(Note: Graphs continued on pages 148 & 149.)
A: For Sunflower Picture, cut one 51 x 100 holes.
B: For Vase and Magazine Box sides, cut six 41 x 90 holes.
C: For Magazine Box front and back, cut two (one for front and one for back) 61 x 90 holes.
D: For Magazine Box bottom, cut one 56 x 76 holes.
E: For Vase bottom, cut one 41 x 41 holes (no graph).

Stitching Instructions:
(Note: E piece is not worked.)
1: Using colors and stitches indicated, work A-D pieces according to graphs, leaving uncoded area unworked. For Sunflower Picture, do not Overcast edges; frame as desired.

2: With red, Whipstitch pieces together as indicated and according to Vase & Magazine Box Assembly Illustration on page 149; Overcast unfinished edges of Vase and Magazine Box.⊛

B – Vase & Magazine Box Side
(cut 6) 41 x 90 holes

COLOR KEY: Sunny Sunflowers

	Worsted-weight	Nylon Plus™	Need-loft®	YARN AMOUNT
■	Red	#20	#01	3½ oz.
▨	White	#01	#41	3 oz.
▨	Straw	#41	#19	70 yds.
■	Forest	#32	#29	30 yds.
▨	Holly	#31	#27	28 yds.
◨	Yellow	#26	#57	25 yds.
▨	Gold	#27	#17	24 yds.
▨	Fern	#57	#23	17 yds.
■	Brown	#36	#15	12 yds.

A – Sunflower Picture
(cut 1)
51 x 100 holes

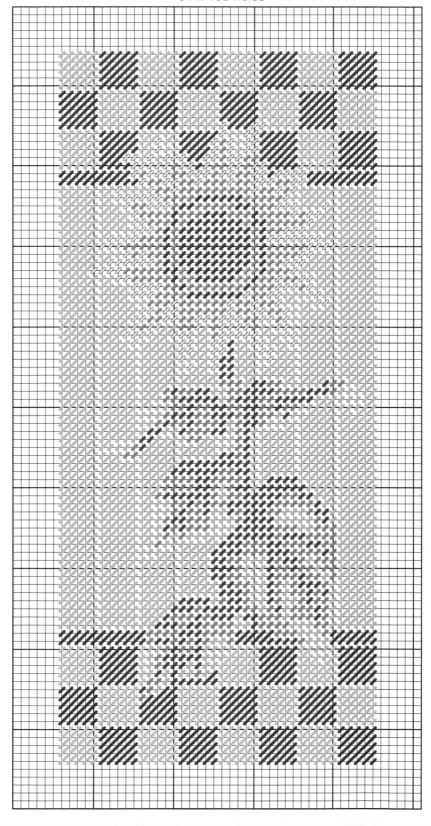

C – Magazine Box Front & Back
(cut 2) 61 x 90 holes

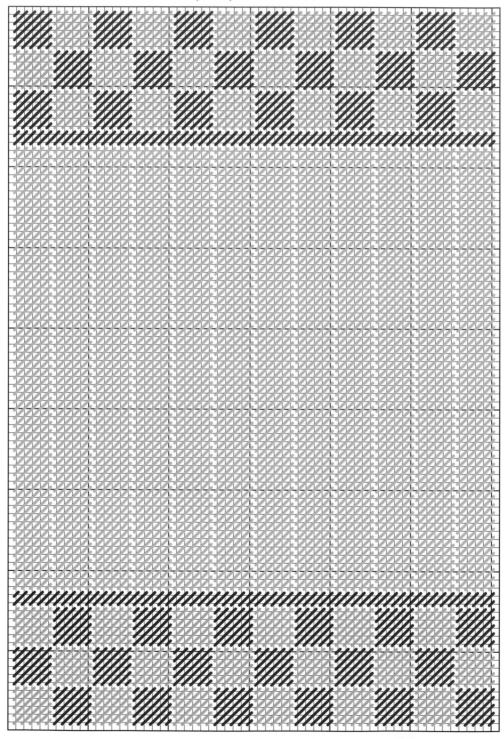

COLOR KEY: Sunny Sunflowers

	Worsted-weight	Nylon Plus™	Need-loft®	YARN AMOUNT
■	Red	#20	#01	3½ oz.
▨	White	#01	#41	3 oz.
▨	Straw	#41	#19	70 yds.
■	Forest	#32	#29	30 yds.
▨	Holly	#31	#27	28 yds.
▨	Yellow	#26	#57	25 yds.
▨	Gold	#27	#17	24 yds.
▨	Fern	#57	#23	17 yds.
■	Brown	#36	#15	12 yds.

STITCH KEY:

☐ Top Assembly Attachment

Vase & Magazine Box Assembly Diagram

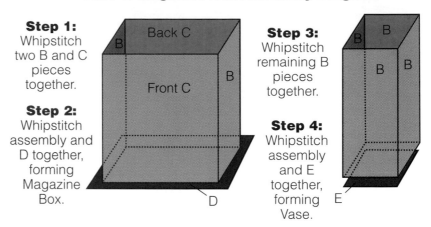

Step 1:
Whipstitch two B and C pieces together.

Step 2:
Whipstitch assembly and D together, forming Magazine Box.

Step 3:
Whipstitch remaining B pieces together.

Step 4:
Whipstitch assembly and E together, forming Vase.

D – Magazine Box Bottom
(cut 1) 56 x 76 holes

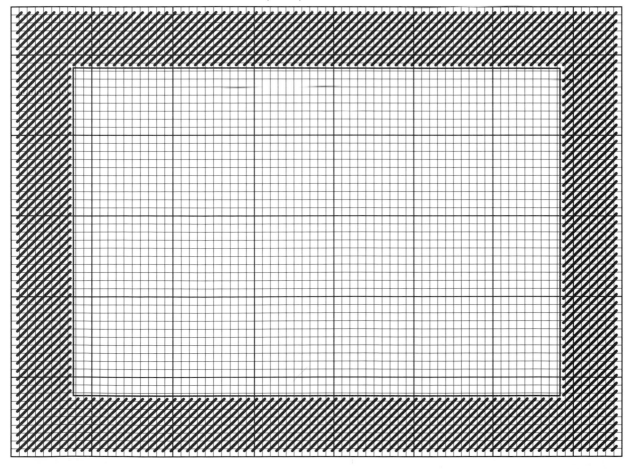

Sports
Pennants

Instructions on page 152

Sports Pennants

Photo on pages 150 & 151.

SIZE & MATERIALS

Sizes: Each is 9¾" x 10⅞".

Materials: Four sheets of 7-count plastic canvas; Worsted-weight or plastic canvas yarn (for amounts see Color Key).

INSTRUCTIONS

Cutting Instructions:

A: For Baseball, cut one according to graph.
B: For Soccer, cut one according to graph.
C: For Basketball, cut one according to graph.
D: For Football, cut one according to graph on page 154.

Stitching Instructions:

1: Using colors and stitches indicated, work pieces according to graphs; with matching colors, as shown in photo, Overcast unfinished edges.
2: Using beige and Straight Stitch, embroider detail on C piece as indicated on graph. Display as desired.❀

COLOR KEY: Sports Pennants

	Worsted-weight	Nylon Plus™	Need-loft®	YARN AMOUNT
	Xmas Green	#58	#28	46 yds.
	Camel	#34	#43	27 yds.
	White	#01	#41	25 yds.
	Moss	#48	#25	14 yds.
	Black	#02	#00	13 yds.
	Pumpkin	#50	#12	11 yds.
	Silver	–	#37	8 yds.
	Bittersweet	#18	#52	7 yds.
	Gray	#23	#38	7 yds.
	Baby Blue	#05	#36	6 yds.
	Cinnamon	#44	#14	6 yds.
	Crimson	#53	#42	5 yds.
	Xmas Red	#19	#02	5 yds.
	Beige	#43	#40	3 yds.
	Brown	#36	#15	3 yds.
	Red	#20	#01	3 yds.
	Royal Dark	#07	#48	3 yds.
	Forest	#32	#29	1 yd.

STITCH KEY:
— Backstitch/Straight Stitch

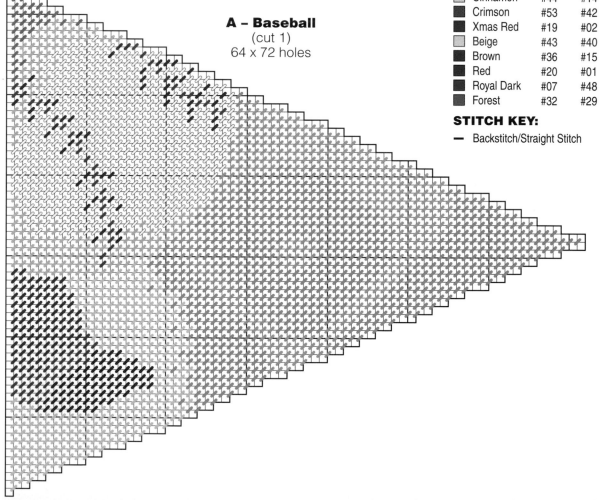

A – Baseball
(cut 1)
64 x 72 holes

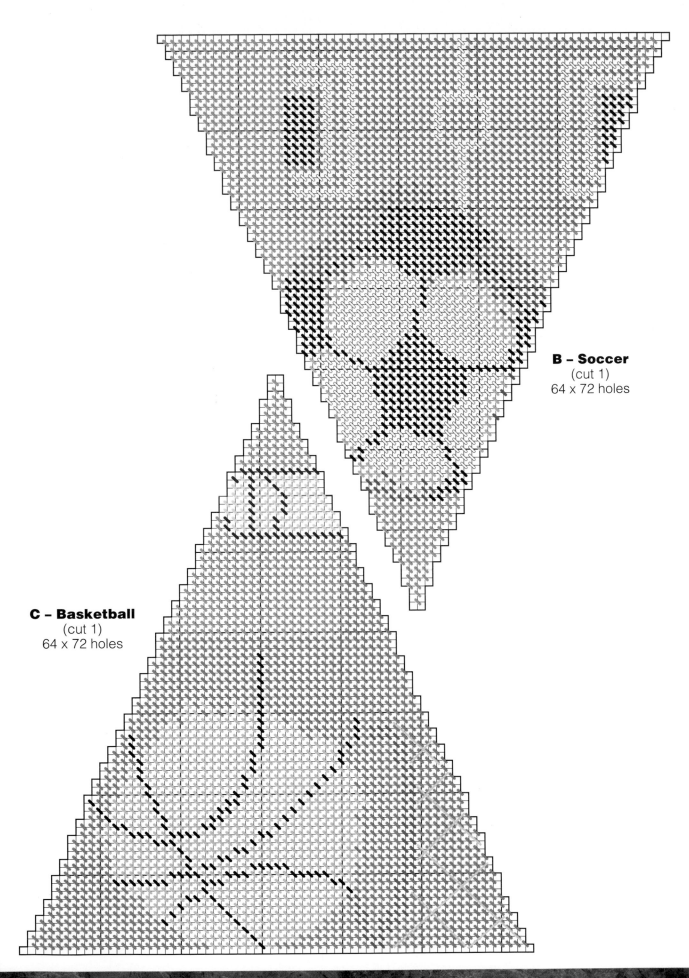

B – Soccer
(cut 1)
64 x 72 holes

C – Basketball
(cut 1)
64 x 72 holes

Sports Pennants

Instructions on page 152.

COLOR KEY: Sports Pennants

Worsted-weight	Nylon Plus™	Need-loft®	YARN AMOUNT
Xmas Green	#58	#28	46 yds.
Camel	#34	#43	27 yds.
White	#01	#41	25 yds.
Moss	#48	#25	14 yds.
Black	#02	#00	13 yds.
Pumpkin	#50	#12	11 yds.
Silver	–	#37	8 yds.
Bittersweet	#18	#52	7 yds.
Gray	#23	#38	7 yds.
Baby Blue	#05	#36	6 yds.
Cinnamon	#44	#14	6 yds.
Crimson	#53	#42	5 yds.
Xmas Red	#19	#02	5 yds.
Beige	#43	#40	3 yds.
Brown	#36	#15	3 yds.
Red	#20	#01	3 yds.
Royal Dark	#07	#48	3 yds.
Forest	#32	#29	1 yd.

D – Football
(cut 1)
64 x 72 holes

General Instructions

Basic Instructions to Get You Started

Most plastic canvas stitchers love getting their projects organized before they even step out the door in search of supplies. A few moments of careful planning can make the creation of your project even more fun.

First of all, prepare your work area. You will need a flat surface for cutting and assembly, and you will need a place to store your materials. Good lighting is essential, and a comfortable chair will make your stitching time even more enjoyable.

Do you plan to make one project, or will you be making several of the same item? A materials list appears at the beginning of each pattern. If you plan to make several of the same item, multiply your materials accordingly. Your shopping list is ready.

Canvas

Most projects can be made using standard-size sheets of canvas. Standard-size sheets of 7-count (7 holes per inch) are always 70 x 90 holes and are about 10½" x 13½". For larger projects, 7-count canvas also comes in 12" x 18" (80 x 120 holes) and 13½" x 22½" (90 x 150 holes) sheets. Other shapes are available in 7-count, including circles, diamonds, purse forms and ovals.

10-count canvas (10 holes per inch) comes only in standard-size sheets, which vary slightly depending on brand. They are 10½" x 13½" (106 x 136 holes) or 11" x 14" (108 x 138 holes).

5-count canvas (5 holes per inch) and 14-count (14 holes per inch) sheets are also available.

Some canvas is soft and pliable, while other canvas is stiffer and more rigid. To prevent canvas from cracking during or after stitching, you'll want to choose pliable canvas for projects that require shaping, like round baskets with curved handles. For easier shaping, warm canvas pieces with a blow-dry hair dryer to soften; dip in cool water to set. If your project is a box or an item that will stand alone, stiffer canvas is more suitable.

Both 7- and 10-count canvas sheets are available in a rainbow of colors. Most designs can be stitched on colored as well as clear canvas. When a pattern does not specify color in the materials list, you can assume clear canvas was used in the photographed model. If you'd like to stitch only a portion of the design, leaving a portion unstitched, use colored canvas to coordinate with yarn colors.

Buy the same brand of canvas for each entire project. Different brands of canvas may differ slightly in the distance between each bar.

Marking & Counting Tools

To avoid wasting canvas, careful cutting of each piece is important. For some pieces with square corners, you might be comfortable cutting the canvas without marking it beforehand. But for pieces with lots of angles and cutouts, you may want to mark your canvas before cutting.

Always count before you mark and cut. To count holes on the graphs, look for the bolder lines showing each ten holes. These ten-count lines begin in the lower left-hand corner of each graph and are on the graph to make counting easier. To count holes on the canvas, you may use your tapestry needle, a toothpick or a plastic hair roller pick. Insert the needle or pick slightly in each hole as you count.

Most stitchers have tried a variety of marking tools and have settled on a favorite, which may be crayon, permanent marker, grease pencil or ball point pen. One of the best marking tools is a fine-point overhead projection marker, available at office supply stores. The ink is dark and easy to see and washes off completely with water. After cutting and before stitching, it's important to remove all marks so they won't stain yarn as you stitch or show through stitches later. Cloth and paper toweling removes grease pencil and crayon marks, as do fabric softener sheets that have already been used in your dryer.

Supplies

Yarn, canvas, needles, cutters and most other supplies needed to complete the projects in this book are available at craft and needlework stores and through mail order catalogs. Other supplies are available at fabric, hardware and discount stores. For mail order information, see page 160.

Cutting Tools

You may find it very helpful to have several tools on hand for cutting canvas. When cutting long, straight sections, scissors, craft cutters or kitchen shears are the fastest and easiest to use. For cutting out detailed areas and trimming nubs, you may like using manicure scissors or nail clippers. Many stitchers love using Ultimate Plastic Canvas Cutters, available only from *The Needlecraft Shop* catalog. If you prefer laying your canvas flat when cutting, try a craft knife and cutting surface – self-healing mats designed for sewing and kitchen cutting boards work well.

Yarn and Other Stitching Materials

You may choose two-ply nylon plastic canvas yarn (the color numbers of two popular brands are found in the general materials lists and Color Keys) or four-ply worsted-weight yarn for stitching on 7-count canvas. There are about 42 yards per ounce of plastic canvas yarn and 50 yards per ounce of worsted-weight yarn.

Worsted-weight yarn is widely available and comes in wool, acrylic, cotton and blends. If you decide to use worsted-weight yarn, choose 100% acrylic for best coverage. Select worsted-weight yarn by color instead of the color names or numbers found in the Color Keys. Projects stitched with worsted-weight yarn often "fuzz" after use. "Fuzz" can be removed by shaving it off with a fabric shaver to make your project look new again.

Plastic canvas yarn comes in about 60 colors and is a favorite of many plastic canvas designers. These yarns "wear" well both while stitching and in the finished product. When buying plastic canvas yarn, shop using the color names or numbers found in the Color Keys, or select colors of your choice.

To cover 5-count canvas, use a doubled strand of worsted-weight or plastic canvas yarn.

Choose sport-weight yarn or #3 pearl cotton for stitching on 10-count canvas. To cover 10-count canvas using six-strand embroidery floss, use 12 strands held together. Single and double plies of yarn will also cover 10-count and can be used for embroidery or accent stitching worked over needlepoint stitches – simply separate worsted-weight yarn into 2-ply or plastic canvas yarn into 1-ply. Nylon plastic canvas yarn does not perform as well as knitting worsted when separated and can be frustrating to use, but it is possible. Just use short lengths, separate into single plies and twist each ply slightly.

Embroidery floss or #5 pearl cotton can also be used for embroidery, and each covers 14-count canvas well.

Metallic cord is a tightly-woven cord that comes in dozens of glittering colors. Some are solid-color metallics, including gold and silver, and some have colors interwoven with gold or silver threads. If your metallic cord has a white core, the core may be removed for super-easy stitching. To do so, cut a length of cord; grasp center core fibers with tweezers or fingertips and pull. Core slips out easily. Though the sparkly look of metallics will add much to your project, you may substitute contrasting colors of yarn.

Natural and synthetic raffia straw will cover 7-count canvas if flattened before stitching. Use short lengths to prevent splitting, and glue ends to prevent unraveling.

Cutting Canvas

Follow all Cutting Instructions, Notes and labels above graphs to cut canvas. Each piece is labeled with a letter of the alphabet. Square-sided pieces are cut according to hole count, and some may not have a graph.

Unlike sewing patterns, graphs are not designed to be used as actual patterns but rather as counting, cutting and stitching guides. Therefore, graphs may not be actual size. Count the holes on the graph (see Marking & Counting Tools on page 155), mark your canvas to match, then cut. The old carpenters' adage – "Measure twice, cut once" – is good advice. Trim off the nubs close to the bar, and trim all corners diagonally.

For large projects, as you cut each piece, it is a good idea to label it with its letter and name. Use sticky labels, or fasten scrap paper notes through the canvas with a twist tie or a quick stitch with a scrap of yarn. To stay organized, you many want to store corresponding pieces together in zip-close bags.

If you want to make several of a favorite design to give as gifts or sell at bazaars, make cutting canvas easier and faster by making a master pattern. From colored canvas, cut out one of each piece required. For duplicates, place the colored canvas on top of clear canvas and cut out. If needed, secure the canvas pieces together with paper fasteners, twist ties or yarn. By using this method, you only have to count from the graphs once.

If you accidentally cut or tear a bar or two on your canvas, don't worry! Boo-boos can usually be repaired in one of several ways: heat the tip of a metal skewer and melt the canvas back together; glue torn bars with a tiny drop of craft glue, super glue or hot glue; or reinforce the torn section with a separate piece of canvas placed at the back of your work. When reinforcing with extra canvas, stitch through both thicknesses.

Stitching the Canvas

Stitching Instructions for each section are found after the Cutting Instructions. First, refer to the illustrations of basic stitches found on page 158 to familiarize yourself with the stitches used. Illustrations will be found near the graphs for pieces worked using special stitches. Follow the numbers on the tiny graph beside the illustration to make each stitch – bring your needle up from the back of the work on odd numbers and down through the front of the work on even numbers.

Before beginning, read the Stitching Instructions to get an overview of what you'll be doing. You'll find that some pieces are stitched using colors and stitches indicated on graphs, and for other pieces you will be given a color and stitch to use to cover the entire piece.

Cut yarn lengths between 18" to 36". Thread needle; do not tie a knot in the end. Bring your needle up through the canvas from the back, leaving a short length of yarn on the wrong side of the canvas. As you begin to stitch, work over this short length of yarn. If you are beginning with Continental Stitches, leave a 1" length, but if you are working longer stitches, leave a longer length.

In order for graph colors to contrast well, graph colors may not match yarn colors. For instance, a light yellow may be selected to represent the metallic cord color gold, or a light blue may represent white yarn.

When following a graph showing several colors, you may want to work all the stitches of one color at the same time. Some stitchers prefer to work with several colors at once by threading each on a separate needle and letting the yarn not being used hang on the wrong side of the work. Either way, remember that strands of yarn run across the wrong side of the work may show through the stitches from the front.

As you stitch, try to maintain an even tension on the yarn. Loose stitches will look uneven, and tight stitches will let the canvas show through. If your yarn twists as you work, you may want to let your needle and yarn hang and untwist occasionally.

When you end a section of stitching or finish a thread, weave the yarn through the back side of your last few stitches, then trim it off.

Needles & Other Stitching Tools

Blunt-end tapestry needles are used for stitching plastic canvas. Choose a No. 16 needle for stitching 5- and 7-count, a No. 18 for stitching 10-count and a No. 24 for stitching 14-count canvas. A small pair of embroidery scissors for snipping yarn is handy. Try using needle-nosed jewelry pliers for pulling the needle through several thicknesses of canvas and out of tight spots too small for your hand.

Construction & Assembly

After all pieces of an item needing assembly are stitched, you will find the order of assembly is listed in the Stitching Instructions and sometimes illustrated in Diagrams found with the graphs. For best results, join pieces in the order written. Refer to the Stitch Key and to the directives near the graphs for precise attachments.

Finishing Tips

To combat glue strings when using a hot glue gun, practice a swirling motion as you work. After placing the drop of glue on your work, lift the gun slightly and swirl to break the stream of glue, as if you were making an ice cream cone. Have a cup of water handy when gluing. For those times that you'll need to touch the glue, first dip your finger into the water just enough to dampen it. This will minimize the glue sticking to your finger, and it will cool and set the glue more quickly.

To attach beads, use a bit more glue to form a cup around the bead. If too much shows after drying, use a craft knife to trim off excess glue.

Scotchguard® or other fabric protectors may be used on your finished projects. However, avoid using a permanent marker if you plan to use a fabric protector, and be sure to remove all other markings before stitching. Fabric protectors can cause markings to bleed, staining yarn.

For More Information

Sometimes even the most experienced needlecrafters can find themselves having trouble following instructions. If you have difficulty completing your project, write to Plastic Canvas Editors, The Needlecraft Shop, 23 Old Pecan Road, Big Sandy, Texas 75755.

NEEDLEPOINT STITCHES

CONTINENTAL STITCH
can be used to stitch designs or fill in background areas.

REVERSE CONTINENTAL STITCH
can be used to stitch designs or fill in background areas.

SCOTCH STITCH
is used to fill in background areas. Stitches cover a square area over three or more bars.

WHIPSTITCH
is used to join two or more pieces together.

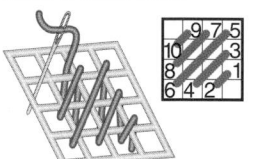

SLANTED GOBELIN STITCH
can be used to stitch designs or fill in background areas. Can be stitched over two or more bars in vertical or horizontal rows.

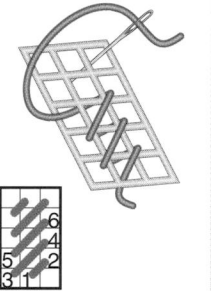

OVERCAST
is used to finish edges. Stitch two or three times in corners for complete coverage.

LONG STITCH
is a horizontal or vertical stitch used to stitch designs or fill in background areas. Can be stitched over two or more bars.

ALTERNATING SLANTED GOBELIN STITCH
can be used to stitch designs or fill in background areas. Can be stitched over two or more bars in vertical or horizontal rows.

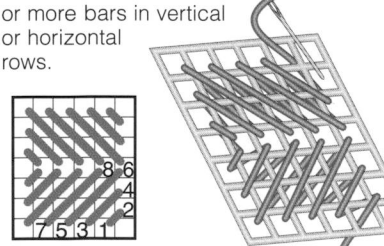

SHEAF STITCH

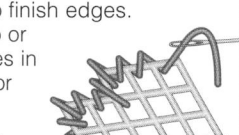

CROSS STITCH
can be used as a needlepoint stitch or as an embroidery stitch stitched over background stitches with contrasting yarn or floss.

MOSAIC STITCH

RYA KNOT STITCH
is used to fill in background areas or as an embroidery stitch to add a loopy or fringed texture. Stitch over two bars leaving a loop, then stitch over the next two bars to anchor the loop.

EMBROIDERY STITCHES

STRAIGHT STITCH
is usually used as an embroidery stitch to add detail. Stitches can be any length and can go in any direction. Looks like Backstitch except stitches do not touch.

LARK'S HEAD KNOT

COUCHING STITCH

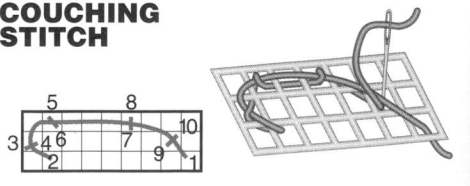

BACKSTITCH
is usually used as an embroidery stitch to outline or add detail. Stitches can be any length and go in any direction.

BEAD ATTACHMENT ILLUSTRATION

FRENCH KNOT
is usually used as an embroidery stitch to add detail. Can be made in one hole or over a bar. If dot on graph is in hole, come up and go down with needle in same hole. If dot is across a bar, come up in one hole and go down one hole over.

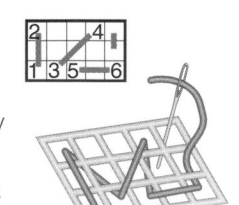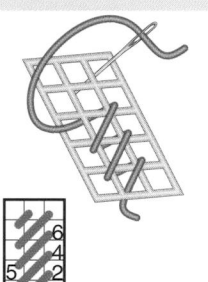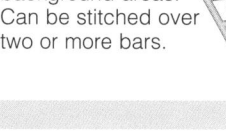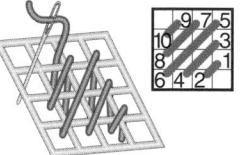

Acknowledgments

We would like to express our appreciation to the many people who helped create this book. Our special thanks go to each of the talented designers who contributed original designs.

We also wish to express our gratitude to the following manufacturers for their generous contribution of materials and supplies for some of the featured projects:

Glenda Chamberlain
Darice® canvas and metallic cord; Needloft® yarn by Uniek® Crafts; and Krenik metallic braid

Janelle Giese of Janelle Marie Designs
Krenik metallic ribbon, braid and cord; DMC® floss and pearl cotton; Needloft® yarn by Uniek® Crafts; and Mill Hill seed beads by Gay Bowles Sales, Inc.

Sandra Miller Maxfield
Darice® canvas, metallic cord, wiggle eyes, plastic coils and gemstones; Needloft® yarn by Uniek® Crafts; and Crafty Magic Melt® glue by Adhesive Technologies, Inc.

Robin Petrina
Darice® canvas, metallic cord and metallic pom-poms; Red Heart® yarn by Coats & Clark®; and Caron® Sayelle® and Simply Soft yarn

Diane T. Ray
Darice® canvas, metallic cord, raffia straw and Nylon Plus™ yarn; Madeira floss; and pony beads from The Beadery®

Mike Vickery
Darice® canvas and metallic cord; and Needloft® yarn by Uniek® Crafts

Michele Wilcox
Darice® canvas; Needloft® yarn by Uniek® Crafts; DMC® pearl cotton; and music box and turntable from National Artcraft Company

Photography Locations & Credits

Photography locations include the homes of Mike and Beth Augustine, Longview, Texas; Bill and Ruth Whitaker, Tyler, Texas; and Charlotte Stevens, *The Sunday House*, Mineola, Texas.

Props provided by *Broadway Florist*, Big Sandy, Texas, and *The Frame Up Gallery*, Tyler, Texas.

Models: Joanna Augustine, Longview, Texas; Micah Godfrey, Big Sandy, Texas; and Stephen, Carolana and Jordan Whitaker, Aldbourne, England.

Pattern Index

For supplies, first shop your local craft and needlework stores. If you are unable to find the supplies you need, write to the address below for a free catalog. The Needlecraft Shop carries plastic canvas in a variety of sizes, plastic canvas yarn and a large selection of pattern books.

23 Old Pecan Road, Big Sandy, Texas 75755 (903) 636-4000 or (800) 259-4000